THE GOOD MANNERS GUIDE

Polite Society:

A voluntary association of persons
committed to maintaining
good manners and courtesy
as the basis of everyday behaviour
in British Society

The Good

Manners Guide

1989

Published by: The Polite Society

First published in 1988 by
THE POLITE SOCIETY
Chairman: Rev. Ian Gregory,
18 The Avenue, Basford,
Newcastle under Lyme, Staffs ST5 0LY

in association with
The Self Publishing Association Ltd
Lloyds Bank Chambers
Upton-upon-Severn
Worcestershire WR8 4HU
England

© Ian Gregory
ISBN 1 85421 021 1 (Hardback)
1 85421 022 X (Paperback)

The Polite Society Logo and other design work was carried out by
Genesis Marketing of Newcastle under Lyme

Typeset by Printit Now Ltd
in Palatino

Printed by Billing & Sons,
Worcester, England

Contents

INTRODUCTION

What are good manners? The answer to that question has depended throughout history on when and where you live.

Good manners in Elizabethan England involved a good deal more formality than we have a taste for today.

Good manners among Jewish people 2,000 years ago was a ritual for which considerable time was required, especially when meeting acquaintances in the street.

Good manners in modern Japan involve a finely-tuned cultural awareness.

Whatever the differences of form dictated by time and place, however, there is a common factor to which men and women of goodwill in every age would consent. Good manners are about treating other people with respect and consideration.

The possession of good manners is the secret of success in almost every area of life.

A restaurant owner discovered that too late. He had acquired a splendid property. He insisted on the highest standards of food, furniture and fittings. He recruited experienced personnel and he set his charges at a fair level.

He went bust.

Why? He said in a letter: "I failed to ensure that the staff knew about courtesy. Word got round that we treated people like dirt."

A small town butcher, on the other hand, could not think why people queued at his shop rather than patronise any of the other butchers' shops in the area. The meat was no better or worse than anybody else's. His was a family business and he could not compete in price with the chain stores or supermarkets. People who shopped with him frequently had to wait. It was left to a customer to explain to him: "It's because we get treated right here."

By that she meant that whenever people went into the shop there was a guarantee of a cheery word, a named welcome, a bit of harmless leg-pulling and a smile-powered conversation.

What all this proves is that above all people want to be treated like human beings. In a world of digits and decibels, software and sociology, people long for respect and recognition that says: you matter.

Good manners lie at the heart of our need. This is especially true in the present age.

In the concluding years of an amazing century when aggression and machismo have fired up the youth of many nations, it has begun to dawn on us that there is a better way to live. Perhaps it is a part of the New Age philosophy that has also given us alternative medicine, meditation and a new interest in religion. The new way can be summed up in the aims and ideals of the Polite Society: in courtesy and consideration for other people.

Let's be honest: a great deal of what passed for courtesy in the days of our Victorian forefathers was not necessarily the good thing that a rose-coloured backward glance makes it out to be. There was a veneer of etiquette on many a family cupboard crammed with skeletons. With one hand a man of breeding might be raising his hat, while with the other he was up to all manner of evil. Morality which had decent people covering up the legs of their dining room tables had little or nothing to say about passions which led to illegitimate children being packed off for life to an asylum. Whatever we now say or think about good manners, it has to be of a better and deeper quality than that.

The best of good manners is not a device for drawing attention to one's mastery of social skills. It is, rather, a self-effacing and genuine wish for the well-being of other people. It is the determination to resist the temptation to revenge. It is a form of self-control of tongue and hand which marks a person out as being different.

The "Good Manners Guide" does not want to take too stringent a moral stance. The Polite Society wants merely to encourage people of goodwill, irrespective of political or religious viewpoint, to hold to a clear pattern of rights and wrongs in terms of courtesy. If you find this book to be about trivial matters, so be it: it is in small civilities and kindnesses that business, traffic, social life, school days and commerce find their sense of meaning and offer their rewards.

There is a struggle going on for the soul of our great country, and this guide is offered for those who want without feeling ashamed to be on the side of the angels. We have a growing multitude of allies, and every polite word or deed is a resounding volley against the vulgarian horde.

Chapter One

A NATIONAL PROBLEM?

The principle has been defined in all the world's great religious systems: Christianity says "whatever you would have people do to you, do you also to them".

Buddhism says: "Hurt not others with that which pains yourself".

Islam says: "Whatever you abhor for yourself, abhor it also for others, and whatever you desire for yourself desire also for others."

Confucianism says: "What you don't want done to yourself, don't do to others".

Hinduism says: "Do naught to others which if done to you would cause you pain".

How these commonly held high principles work out in daily life is the substance of courtesy.

A wide range of cultural and religious backgrounds now forms the population of the United Kingdom. The pattern of daily life here has absorbed over the last 50 years many different attitudes and feelings about life, other people, home, work, religion, education and trade. Those who were born and brought up here have observed habits of life and customs which are alien to them, and it is greatly to the credit of most communities that these things have generally been accepted with goodwill and understanding.

Humour should not be under-estimated in any discussion about good manners. The fine balance between offence and tolerance among individuals and groups is often tilted by a lighthearted remark, although even humour has its regional and international variations. In spite of all these differences in human disposition, basic good manners will be recognised and appreciated throughout the world. In every race men and women want to be appreciated, treated with kindness and valued as individuals.

The British are an old and experienced people. Much of our reputation over the centuries has depended on the way we treated others. The Empire developed through a variety of strategies, not all of them to our credit, but the best of our representatives' behaviour was splendid, and happily there are pockets of communal life throughout the world where Great Britain is regarded with genuine affection because some trader, teacher, serviceman or preacher demonstrated by a habit of life and speech the fundamentals of courtesy.

Keith Waterhouse, writing in the Daily Mail, has vividly pictured the real struggle taking place in British society at the end of this century, as one between the well and ill-mannered.

Is that over-stating the case? There is a form of universal despair about the overt bad behaviour of many people in private and in public. The lout who puts his/her feet on the railway carriage seat, throws chip papers into the gutter, belches and bellows, sneers and leers at passers by, is a common phenomenon. So, sadly now of the sportsground hooligan, he is one step removed from creatures kept behind bars at the zoo, whose social and personal conduct may in fact be far more acceptable to their kind.

Bad behaviour by mobs is nothing new to this country. Every age has produced ill-mannered strata from top to bottom of the social tapestry. Among lower orders it was thought to originate in poor education, bad housing, poverty and unemployment. There was a genuine expectation at the start of this century that when conditions of everyday life improved, general behaviour would be better in every way, and crime would disappear.

When Lord Lane, the Lord Chief Justice, opened new Court accommodation in Manchester in 1987, he recalled this hope. He reminded his audience that we now had an Education Act, clean air, better housing and improved working conditions. Yet it was now required of society that more accommodation must be found in prison. In spite of the much better conditions of life, and the affluence of most people compared to the conditions in which their grandparents lived, people had no respect for the property or person of their neighbours.

Lord Lane might have added a range of other ways in

which life has improved for the average citizen of the United Kingdom. For all its shortcomings we have a National Health Service. There are much shorter working hours. The world is open for easier and cheaper travel. We have six national parks to enjoy in our own country. Let the list roll on: clean, reliable water, wide roads, public transport, nicer fabrics for our clothes, expertise readily available on many subjects from home cooking to clearing up acne. One old lady in a warden controlled bungalow told a volunteer helper that she was sorry not to be able to accept his invitation to attend a bingo session: she had a hair appointment at noon, and the chiropodist was coming at 4.00 p.m. – all for a very small cost.

If life offers all these benefits, why are we not happier, better, more contented men and women, willing to be nice to one another?

There are as many opinions about the reason for our malaise as there are people walking about in the street, sitting in the bar parlour, or attending their local church. A personal view is that we have been encouraged to have a much greater expectation of life than ever before. My grandmother never saw the sea, nor did she ever go to London. She had no wish to do either of these things, and she thought a trip by tram into Manchester town centre six miles away from her back street terraced home excitement enough for any self-respecting woman. She was content with a life firmly anchored to a restricted routine: keeping the house clean; yellow-stoning the front step, boiling up the stewpot, and caring for her children.

These children were not going to be satisfied with the same kind of life. They made whoopee at the local church hall, took charabanc trips to Blackpool, went to war in distant places, became experts on the tourist route round London, and thought about going to Paris for the weekend.

A watershed in inter-personal relationships was reached when THEIR children came on the scene, around 1950. All the cultural and spiritual markers were ripped up and thown out along with every other hangover from the past.

Television began to portray the world as a Mecca, all set about by glamour, comfort, and excitement. This good life, we all decided, was for us. The message was reinforced by glossy magazines, whose enhanced printing techniques displayed homes, holidays, gardens, sexual delights of which our predecessors only knew as whispered rumour from a world of pure fantasy. Now, to our amazement, we saw that these things were real. Voices from the recesses of advertising studios told us that it could all be ours.

By instinct human nature wants all the good things within reach, and traditional good manners have been swept aside in the stampede to grab a share of all these wonderful modern advantages.

Also out of the window have gone many other virtues: modesty, fidelity, scrupulous honesty and simplicity among them.

Nobody wants to go back to "the old days" even if it were possible. We want to retain the high standard of living we now enjoy. The price we have to pay for "progress" however, appears to be the decline of good manners. We have to accept that there will be pushing and shoving, grabbing and grasping, jealousy and back-biting, spite and double dealing.

The success story of our time appears on the face of it to require old fashioned virtues to be abandoned. As Singapore's second deputy Premier Mr Rajaratnam, has pointed out, it is easy for "moneytheism" to become the accepted religion, and in the worship of such a god selfishness rules. To think otherwise is to indicate ignorance of what is really happening in today's world.

Waterhouse may be right: many who do not like what they see of this world and its crumbled values have tended to think that the only thing to do is to retreat behind the lace curtains and cluck their tongues in disgust. Until now there was nothing else that could be done.

Times, however, do change. Trends in social behaviour alter as generations rise and fall, and new perceptions are opened up. Now the forces which favour good manners and better inter-personal behaviour are rallying. Young people especially are interested in a different kind of lifestyle from what has upset them in their elders during the last 20 years. When the Polite Society asked children to come up with ideas for a junior code of courtesy there were several hundred suggestions – from a small number of children at schools who had thought the thing through themselves. Therefore, all is not lost.

Fortunately the senior management of many a firm is beginning to make the greatest discovery of our century: that manners matter. It is a commercial, economic fact.

You go to an hotel where the food is excellent, the furnishing of high quality, the fittings and facilities are first class. But you are not happy. You try to analyse it. In the end you discover the reason: nobody cares whether you are there or not.

You do not go back to that place, if you can help it. You may instead go to the hotel where the food is less than cordon bleu, the style is slightly shabby, and the decor wilting. But when you go in somebody smiles, remembers your name, and takes a serious interest in you as a person. We are now discovering that when we have got the product or service as good as it can conceivably be, all the publicity right, with words and pictures as sharp as needles, we can still go wrong. Why? Because we have not paid enough attention to personal relationships.

The Managing Director of Peebles Hydro, Scotland, Peter van Dijk, told me that guests go back year after year to his superb hotel. The weather may be bad, and just occasionally the problems of running a big hotel are evident. But people return because they are cherished and made welcome.

Public relations in this country has only just started to realise this. For too long we have depended on words and pictures to put over our products and services. Now we need to see that our salesmen, engineers, counter staff, telephonists, and everybody to do with our firm, shop, restaurant, knows how to present a good, clean, confident image. To quote but a few examples:

Among the thousands of letters written in response to the formation of the Polite Society was one from a man who said he found real enjoyment in his work now that he was having to deal with people rather than a production conveyor belt where for 20 years he had earned a high wage. "There is a harmony and satisfaction in forming good and helpful relationships that you don't get from machinery," he wrote. He was for the first time in his life a successful human being. He had become a funeral director.

Greengrocer John Ingall, of Nottinghamshire, got the "edge" over supermarkets in his area which at one time threatened to price him into difficulties. He put out a sign which said: "In this shop we say please and thank you." He joined the Polite Society and said in a letter that his business had become very good ever since he put out the sign.

Many firms, supermarket chains, hotel groups, public service industries and airlines among others are now calling in courtesy consultants to encourage their staff to be "customer friendly." Mansfield Inns of Nottinghamshire, introduced a training scheme for many of their 300 plus pubs and hotels. They knew the day had come on which they could no longer improve significantly on the quality of their beer, their furniture, their fittings. The area in which they could get an advantage over their competitors was in the way people were treated when they came into the premises. They called in Polite Society inspectors to assess the difference their training scheme had made.

After a training course in customer care run by the Polite Society a shop assistant told her family that she was getting through her days with far less hassle than ever before. People were found to be much more agreeable to her and at the end of the working day, she was actually less tired than she had been prior to the course. She looked and felt better. Her social life was truly enjoyable. Her wise mother observed: "It's no wonder: you have started working with the forces of life and not against them."

Spotted by member Trevor Wilford in Reader's Digest:

> "We need more people to stand up and protest when something happens that they think is wrong. We need more people who are prepared to raise an objection to loutish, offensive or inconsiderate behaviour on the part of others in public places. We need more people who are willing to become self-styled teachers of those who have no other way of learning what it right, and what is wrong: what is acceptable and what unacceptable."

Stephen Pimenoff in The Guardian

Chapter Two

PRACTICAL MANNERS

Being polite is a passport to a much more satisfactory and successful life. The best reason for good manners is that it helps other people to get through their day. But the spin off for our personal benefit is immense.

The well mannered person has a 100 per cent advantage over aggressive, surly characters in almost every area of life.

I have no doubt that they will have a happier working day. Career prospects are far better. They will make and keep friends. They are less likely to be ill, mentally, spiritually and physically, because they are working in harmony with basic life forces instead of against them.

It has not yet dawned on the macho multitudes of sullen self-conscious young men who haunt pubs and clubs the land over that what they are looking for and paying so much for – the respect and admiration of the prettiest girls – is much more easily accessible by being polite. Women of all ages are longing to meet somebody who will just treat them with gentleness and consideration. A very attractive 18 year old told me in despair that all the boys she knew seemed to be loud mouthed semi-idiots, who had no idea how to engage in conversation or treat people with simple kindness.

So in personal relationships, those who wish to be successful, over a café table, over a counter, in business and social life, should first ask: DO I LIKE PEOPLE? Perhaps they should go one step further back and ask: DO I LIKE ME?

Self-respect is a vital ingredient of any successful person – in their home, school, office or free time. If people are permanently aware of their own shortcomings they are by nature unattractive.

Remember that other people become aware of your existence at three levels: what they SEE, what they HEAR, and what they FEEL ABOUT YOU.

Spend some time thinking about each of these things. When people look at you, what do they see? 1) They see POSTURE.

It is perhaps a sign of our increasing dependence on wheeled transport that we are losing the art of just standing and walking. Perhaps we should not expect RADA standards of deportment, but there are simple ways in which we can all improve our general posture in relation to other people. We have been brought through evolution to a position where we are expected to stand up straight on two legs. Unless we are in some way handicapped, we are intended to stand straight, with shoulders back and head erect.

Try it. Practise it. Stand in front of the mirror and make yourself two inches taller. Look in shop windows and see how you are doing as you walk along. If you have self confidence and self respect it will show in your stance.

Study the way other people stand. Watch them in bus queues, waiting to be served in shops, standing at bars, talking in the street. How much slouching, shuffling and fidgeting there is!

This century has also seen the decline of walking as a human art. Perhaps Henry T Ford is to blame most of all, for giving us the idea that we are mainly intended to move from place to place on wheels. A great deal of time and energy is devoted to skill in other areas of excellence: swimming, playing games, jogging are hugely popular sports. But I have seen a dolphin-like swimmer haul himself out of the water and lurch around the pool as if he could not walk properly at all. The way we walk makes a deep subconscious impression on others. They base their reaction to us on many things, but high among them is how they see us move about in ordinary life. We may shuffle, lope, trot, or slouch. Be sure your walk will find you out.

What is it about the spare parts department of garages that brings out the worst in human deportment? I am indebted to Polite Society member Geoffrey Browne for the observation that in every one of these places there is normally an overalled character spreadeagled over the counter trying to express himself in motor jargon. Here is "automotive man" with spine weakened by years of addiction to driving about behind the wheel of a car. Is it too cynical to suggest that evolution will eventually give us vast big ends, and permanently curved spines, to make it easier for us to sit in our vehicles?

Most of us need to slow down our walking pace, take longer strides, stand straight and swing along as naturally as we can.

People also become aware of us through our facial expression.

We cannot help the face with which we were born. But we can help what we do with it. The ugliest old lady I ever saw was the most beautiful person I ever knew.

There are many people about who have been gifted with superb facial features. Normally they are aware of it and spend much time and money trying to improve this perfection, and holding back the wonderful process of its maturing and ageing. What they are not aware of is the incalculable improvement that can be made to any face by teaching it to smile.

An easy smile is a gift. But we can train ourselves in smile-technique. It comes best to those who are inwardly relaxed and self confident. I would say that a smile is the present God gives to us when we have said Good Day to Him in prayer. An easy smile involves the whole face, including mouth and eyes. The false smile uses only the mouth. A fixed smile is unnerving! Do not switch a smile on and off like a fairy light: it is deeply confusing.

We need also to look as healthy as we can. A doctor's

first act on diagnosing his patient is to look at his/her face – it offers many clues. So to we owe it to our family, friends, customers to be and look as well as we can. Hangovers and other signs of dissipation are soon detected, and are a sure let-down. Make-up is a matter for personal taste, although there is enough advice available, surely!

Take trouble about being and staying clean. No amount of cosmetics will mask for long the sight and smell of a person who is less than thoroughly clean at the start of the day. It applies to body and clothes, and it applies to teeth. Bad breath is fatal. Somebody once said that halitosis was better than no breath at all – but only marginally. Keep in touch with your dentist.

A frequently neglected feature of cleanliness is shoes. Even modestly priced shoes can be kep clean, and thought should be given to whether, with the amazing variety of footware now available, what you propose to wear is appropriate for the event.

What about dress? Employers sometimes expect people to wear uniforms, and in that case the only problem is keeping the clothing clean and well pressed. Otherwise, remember that what you wear speaks volumes about who you are. Clothes are a firm statement about personality. Perhaps they are an attempt to hide insecurity, or an extension of natural exuberance. Gone are the days when people had a small wardrobe of clothes that were expected to last for years. Now more people dress according to personal taste and current fashion. Chain stores are not the only source of wearable clothes. My own daughter – a lively teenager – dresses to great effect from "swap shops" and charity stores. A quick rule of thumb is to ask what people are likely to think about you when they see you looking like that? Are you over or under-stating yourself? Are you embarrassing other people? Is what you wear really telling the world the sort of thing you want the world to hear?

Eye contact is another obvious but underdeveloped gift in personal relationships. Look at people when they are talking to you and you are talking to them. By that I do not mean look at their mouth, or their nose, their hair, or their ears: but at their eyes. In conversation the temptation is to look at paperwork, hands, money, something you are selling, some other person, or just generally to gaze around. Overcome this! Stop everything when somebody speaks to you and listen with evident attention, maintaining eye contact as much as possible. If you like, incline your whole body slightly towards them to indicate that they have your full and individed attention.

The way we use our hands is a key indication of our mood and attitude to other people. Keep them clean, especially finger nails. It is not a good idea to appear with lumps of sticking plaster all over one's fingers, unless there has been some recent accident! Do not wear a dazzling range of rings and ornaments: hands are tools for work, and need the minimum decoration. In conversation there is no need to flap them about needlessly: try to let your voice do the talking. Men should not shake hands with women unless the woman offers her hand first.

Now let us turn to what people HEAR from you.

Let us be clear that the Polite Society is not promoting JUNK civility. What we say should be considered, and meant. But a lot depends on HOW we say things.

Speak clearly and don't rush what you have to say. Two of the biggest faults in daily conversation are mumbling, and shouting. Study your own speech, and try to guess where you are on a personal communication scale of 1 to 10, one being a low mumble, and 10 being a permanent yell. Next try to modify it until you are speaking clearly, plainly, audibly, at around 4 to 6. There are so many tape recorders around now this should be an easy and certainly rewarding exercise. As a BBC radio producer for ten years, I know how amazed people are when they hear their own voices for the first time: most of us have no idea what we sound like, and with a little concentrated effort, everybody can train to sound better.

Nobody should worry about a regional accent, unless it is very pronounced and unpleasant. What is the matter with a voice that announces our place of origin? As long as we can be understood, an accent can be a pleasant and interesting aspect of personality. Woe to us when our regional variations have been filtered out and we are all speaking a bland London suburban.

I make no apology for claiming that the most important part of any conversation is LISTENING to what somebody else is saying. It is almost a lost art, exemplified for ever by the late Mr Al Read, whose sketch of two women talking over the fence was social comment at its highest. Plainly, neither was paying the slightest attention to the other, and only using the occasion to bounce bits of gossip off the other.

My grandmother's weekly letter also epitomised one-way thinking. She wrote a short note every week which always ended: "Hoping this finds you as it leaves me – not too well at present". Her solicitous good wishes, even, were an opportunity to say something about her own condition.

As we are not normally trained to listen, and when we are we earn the esoteric title "counsellor", it will repay close and disciplined attention. One who can really listen will be miles ahead of the game, at work and play, in our time.

Many of the people we meet in our daily lives are shy, uncertain, and diffident. If they are shouting and aggressive it is because nobody has paid much attention to them, and they have to assert themselves to get a word in. If they meet in you one who will actually listen, you are a monarch in the art of relationship.

Pay attention, and concentrate. If you are not sure what is being said or meant, do not be shy to ask for clarification.

Never neglect an opportunity to say "please" and "thank you". Do not be obsequious and over-do it, but say these words as if you mean them. Under stress it is possible to say these valuable words in an off-hand way or even to forget to say them at all. That is like keeping your jewels in a bank vault where nobody ever sees them! We should try not to abbreviate our thanks by saying "ta" or even worse, "cheers". Just say "thank you".

A great deal of what passes for courtesy may be fashionable social habit. There is nothing wrong with the American "Have a nice day" if it is sincerely meant. "Have a good day" would be better because "nice" is a yukky kind of word without much meaning. If you happen to know that somebody is off on holiday part from them with a reference to that. "Have a good time in Skegness", sounds fine. Or: "I hope you find your grandmother better" or "Have a safe journey to Manchester". Try to be specific about something, as it demonstrates that you have been listening.

We have all experienced sensations of attraction or repulsion in the presence of other people. Before they have said a word we develop a feeling about them. It has to do with how they look, and the way they look at us, but I believe it has much more to do with incompatible frequencies which human beings sometimes encounter.

The world of biology has been stimulated of late by the ideas of Rupert Sheldrake, who is showing us the possibility of a totally new way of thinking about the way living entities are formed.* He suggests that there is a "field" for every kind of life form, which accounts for the reason why things develop into carrots or cabbages, mice or people. This is consistent with the view long held that each of us has an "aura" – an invisible but nonetheless real energy field all around us, which is recognisable by other people by means other than the five senses.

If this is true, and something like it must be, then we need to consider carefully what we are saying that nobody "sees" or "hears". From the day of our birth we are sending out "messages" about ourselves, communicating by scream, grunt, mutter, posture, look, or mood. The actual words we use are in the end only a minor part of what we are really saying.

The way we sit, whether we fidget, whether and how we fold our arms or cross our legs, the wringing of hands or constant fiddling with money in a pocket or a key ring, or chewing a pencil, shrugging, leaning back with hands behind the head, nodding, shaking the head, the infinite ways we use the muscles of the face to express a feeling . . . all these things send out definite messages. How close we stand to people, what we allow to come between us when we converse, like a chair or a desk, whether we really are relaxed or mentally tight, all do the same.

We can do very little to correct "bad vibes" which we give to some people, because to a large extent they are beyond our control, just as is the colour of our hair or the pattern of our features. There is just one thing we can do, though, and it will certainly help: we can take time to like people. If we are genuinely caring and interested personalities, it will always show, and the vibes will never be so bad as if we wake up each day resenting that the world has so many people in it who are like us.

* A New Science of Life. Paladin 1987

Streetnice

Polite people may be "streetwise" but they are also "streetnice", in that they think about the impact they are having on the well-being of others, as they walk about.

It is now common to see people eating and drinking in the street, and this is socially intolerable. Fish and chips may taste nicer from a newspaper, but the resultant hideous litter is one reason why our country at weekends resembles a take-away battleground. We are all the casualties, as to drop litter is a gesture of contempt for society at large. Eating and drinking should be reserved, whenever possible, for a designated locale like ones dining room, a café, restaurant, pub, or picnic area.

In smaller towns and villages where people often meet friends when they are out and about, it frequently happens that groups gather on the pavement. This prevents the free flow of other folk along the pavement, and is especially difficult for parents with prams. When you meet friends, draw them into a place where no obstruction will be caused to others before you start a conversation.

The use of umbrellas in the street or at an event where crowds are present is a skill in its own right. The simple rule is to do nothing that would obstruct the view or the passageway or any other person.

Do not hover about in shop doorways: others may be trying to get in or out. By the same measure shopkeepers should not crowd the pavement outside their premises with goods for sale. Uninterrupted access at all times should be the aim, both past the premises and within them.

Crossing the street at traffic lights should be dictated at all times by the "green man" or a traffic warden. Avoid dashing over the street in a way that might confuse passing drivers or cyclists and giving a very bad example to other people who may not be so nimble.

Kindly, polite people stand at the mirror before they go out every morning and practise their smiles. A relaxed face, an easy and slow walking pace, a willingness at once to go to the help of anybody in distress are the marks of a courteous person. These things cost nothing, as is the case with courtesy in any context, but could make going out and about much more of a pleasure than a chore.

Manners in the office

During the years of our working life we spend up to eight hours every day in the company of other people who are colleagues in the same area of endeavour. So we might as well make up our minds to make the most of our time in the office, and that won't happen if it is a place of snarling bad temper, surly behaviour and point-scoring.

In the average office of our European friends members of the staff can spend a good part of every day in greeting one another. The handshakes all-round have much to commend them, but it is perhaps sadly not part of our cultural tradition to engage in such habits. However, there is nothing to beat a cheery "Good morning" and a comment about the traffic, the weather, last night's TV or people's state of health to break the day in gently.

The atmosphere in every office is different, but the furniture and equipment may be similar. It is subtly controlled by one or two strong personalities who dictate whether the daily routine of going to work is pleasant or a chore. To those in a subordinate position, there are attitudes to take which can all the same keep there are attitudes to take which can all the same keep the mood pleasant and the productivity high. Adlai Stevenson, the American diplomat, once put it like this: "To act coolly, intelligently and prudently in perilous circumstances is the test of man," to which we would only add: and woman.

As an employee, one should try to arrive on time and not to spend ages in the loo, or in private conversation before settling at one's desk. An office manager once said that to double the work output of his one-girl office he would need to take on two others, because just one more would give the first girl somebody to talk to all day, and the output would actually fall.

It is important to get to know the chain of command in the office structure, and to do what you are told, with good grace, even though it may seem inconvenient or unnecessary.

Superiors worth their salt will always be pleased to hear of time-saving ideas or suggestions about how office functions can be performed more effectively. If you have an idea, air it.

If you are left to get on with some work for long periods of time, do it as conscientiously as you can. In today's offices there is little time for managers to walk round supervising staff.

If people are leaving for any reason, be prepared cheerfully to make a donation towards a leaving present. I am a firm believer in an office kitty to which all staff in each section should contribute now and donated to some 30 leaving presents found when he left that there were only two people left for his final fling.

Do not gossip about other members of the staff behind their backs. It is all very well saying this, of course, but much harder to keep to the rule. If somebody is not pulling their weight, or is dishonest, or flirting with some other employee, ignore it unless it threatens to disrupt the efficiency of the company. You then must tell a senior member of staff. Try not to write memos: they are easily lost and may stray into the wrong hands.

On the telephone, try to speak with a smile in the voice. Never sound as if you are in such a hurry that you have no time for the caller. Speak slowly and cheerfully. Always thank people who return your call. Be clear in giving your name, and listen carefully to the name of the other party. Jot it down in case you forget it, and use it when you say goodbye.

What about the situation when you have a message for somebody in your office who is engaged on a long telephone call? It is not a good idea to stand within eye contact, waving. Put a written note on the desk in front of them.

At meetings, try to be prepared with all the information that you envisage may be needed. Get there early. Remember nobody can ever be "on time" because the moment at which it is exactly half past ten is so fleeting you will always be early or late. Be early.

37

If you have to address the meeting, do it through the chairman, and at all times keep calm. Never let emotion take over.

Make sure your watch or paging system does not go off during a meeting. I sometimes think that the whole world spends its time, perhaps wastes its time is more accurate, at meetings. If we could learn to stick to the point and abbreviate what we have to say to those things that are essential we could release a tremendous amount of time for more productive activities.

As in every other area of life, the watchword in the office is consideration for others. There will be many times when other people will lose their tempers, moan and complain about something or somebody. You can easily become a part of this negative syndrome, and then wonder why you go home tired, depressed and feeling unfulfilled. If you have done your share, looked your best, remained cheerful through adversity, left your office desk clear, and had a refreshing but not over-indulgent lunch break, you will get home ready for anything and feeling fine.

Travelling

By train: wait until everybody has got off before you get on. Never push through a crowd of alighting passengers, it is dangerous and aggravating.

If the train is full, occupy one seat only. You have

paid for that seat, not the one next to it, so don't put a coat or bag there as if it is reserved for somebody else when it is not.

Don't put your feet on the seat in front of you. It makes the seat dirty and wears out the fabric.

Do not play loud music on your cassette player; get a personal stereo.

Only smoke in clearly defined smoking areas.

In the toilets, leave the facilities as clean as you would expect to find them.

Wait until the train stops before opening doors to alight: people waiting on the platform could be hurt.

By bus: If you are a youngish and more or less fit, and a person who is old or handicapped is standing, give up your seat to them with a cheery smile. Similarly, give your seat to a mother with a child, or anybody struggling with heavy parcels. Children should be prepared to stand so that adults can sit down.

Have your fare ready for the driver as you board – preferably the right amount if you know what it is. Arm yourself with change beforehand. Nothing delays the journey more than to ask the driver for a 45p ticket and offer him a ten pound note. Get up in good time to alight as the bus approaches your stop. Never distract the driver while the bus is in motion. The same applies on buses as on trains: no loud music or feet on seats.

Other areas of daily life will be considered in future 'Good Manners Guides'. Suggestions will be welcomed.

Food for thought...

"I'm the fellow who goes into a restaurant, sits down patiently and waits while the waitresses do everything except take my order.
I'm the fellow who goes into a store, and stands quietly while the salesgirls finish their chat.
I'm the man who drives into a petrol station and never blows his horn but waits patiently while the attendant finishes reading his comic.
Yes, you might say I'm a good guy.
But do you know who else I am?
I'm the fellow who never comes back. And it amuses me to see you spending thousands of pounds every year in advertising to get me back, when I was there in the first place and all you had to do was to show me a little courtesy."
(With acknowledgments to whoever wrote it).

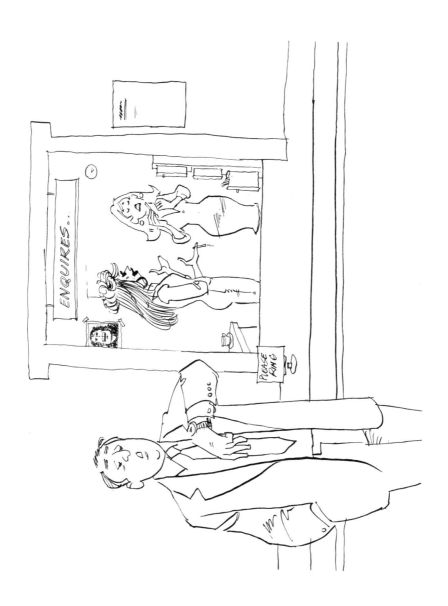

41

Chapter Three

DOCTORS, BARMEN, CLERGY

To hear what hundreds of people report about the way they are treated by the medical profession is to wonder whether some doctors are not among the most brusque, self-appointed divinities in modern society. Of course we do not mean ALL doctors. I asked a good number of people at random what they thought of their doctor and more than half said they were well satisfied with the service they receive.

Some said they regarded their doctor as their only friend, and one woman wrote: "If it had not been for him my life would not have been worth living these past 20 years". A considerable number of people said they did not know their doctor, because happily they have managed to get by for a long period of time without having to consult him or her professionally.

It is the minority who worry me. One woman wrote and said that for no reason she could think of her doctor was simply rude to her. "I do not go to bother him much, for I know how busy they are. But when I had to go he told me to go away and stop wasting his time," she wrote. "I was so amazed that for some days

I could hardly speak."

Another woman told how her doctor gave her two minutes of his time, diagnosed sciatica, and without any conversation scribbled a prescription. She was eventually told that she had cancer.

When I mentioned publicly that most complaints from those who have written to the Polite Society were about the way people are treated by their doctors, it was as if flood gates opened. By telephone and letter dozens of local people wanted to tell me of horrific ordeals, of dismissive treatment, and of a feeling of being totally ignored by their medical practitioner. "I told my doctor that I wanted to have another view about my health, and in the post next day I got a letter telling me to find another GP," said one lady.

A man told me he felt so poorly that he thought he would go to the local surgery for the first time in years and see what might be wrong. "The place was closed: not even a receptionist was on duty. But there was a cleaner, and by the time I had talked to her for half an hour I felt so much better I didn't need the doctor."

The first thing to be said about all this is that doctors are certainly under a great deal of pressure. But not so much as they like us to think. When Paul Ferris wrote his book The Doctors (Gollancz 1965) he spoke of many of them relishing the thought that they were a race apart, taking the place in modern society that the priest once held.

Ferris wrote then, "One day patients will not run the present risk of being pushed around by hospitals – kept waiting, ticked off, left in doubt and generally treated as though they were somehow an impediment to the otherwise smooth running of the institution. Now that doctors are not so dependent on magical qualities, perhaps they will become less authoritarian and less aloof from their patients." Was he being too optimistic?

Very happily, a number of doctors have invited Polite Society inspectors to study the way they run their practices. In every case the practice concerned had built up an outstanding local reputation for the greatest possible care and concern for their patients. Receptionists are also being offered training in the management of medical practices. It is a complicated enough world anyway, but the development of a good relationship with patients is of the highest priority, and it is encouraged to think that the message is getting through.

But let nobody forget the role of the vulgar, demanding, unpleasant and grumpy patient in all this. Since I began to look into this question, I have been told hair-raising stories of aggressive and loud-mouthed patients who demand attention with no trace of restraint, as if they had some divine right to immediate attention and expensive service. "No doubt they are worried and anxious, but they have a very peculiar way of showing it sometimes," said one receptionist. "I have heard abusive and filthy language on the telephone and face to face that has sent me home weeping." Offering any sort of public service these days is, it seems, a risky enterprise.

There have been some sad stories, too, about the treatment people have received at the hands of public officials in housing departments, rates offices, and DHSS centres. Some public house licensees have given offence by surly and ungracious attitudes. But a barman in Stoke on Trent came back pretty sharply at this criticism. Mr I.D. Vernon said:

"The vast majority of customers are bad mannered. I do not hesitate either to use the expression 'vast majority.' Seldom do we hear the words 'please' or 'thank you', and we have abuse hurled at us when it is busy. We have empty glasses thrust under our noses with demands for 'pint o' lager'. Glasses are hammered on the bar for service and 'ay' seems to be the most popular way of addressing people. Abuse and threats at closing time are also common. The few polite people we serve are a pleasure to look after, and if all people treated us with good manners and patience we would feel more good will in return. People in tatty jeans can be extremely polite, while businessmen in their fancy suits and cars can be extremely rude. I nominate bar staff as the group of people at the receiving end of the worst manners from the public."

The surprise among critical letters, however, was about some ungracious clergymen. I know from personal experience what an impossible job the clergyman is trying to do. He (or she) has to be all things to all men. Some are workaholics and never have time for relaxation, which tends to make them crusty. Some are totally disorganised and are not sure what their role is or what they should be doing next. Others are aggressively certain that they are right and everybody else is wrong. It is hardly possible to discuss deep human problems with ministers in any of these categories. The majority of ordained ministers have lived with failure and rejection for so long that it is some kind of miracle when one of them retains a calm serenity, and the gift of being a good listener, into middle and later years.

There have been a significant number of letters, all the same, about clergymen who on the face of it could have controlled themselves better or been more prepared to listen to what they were being told. Some were obviously hiding behind rules which they said had been laid down for them or they had made up themselves, to decline a service of baptism, or a wedding. I say nothing about the reasons for such attitudes. What has caused such offence, however, is the abrupt and curt way some people have been treated. Clergymen may be exhausted, baffled, disappointed, and fed up with the apparently stupid people they have to deal with. But there can be no excuse for arrogance, or treating them as if they were nuisances. Again, a small minority among a vast army of saintly people. But it should not happen at all.

"I have started wearing a hat. This is not a startling announcement, so let me explain just why I've bought a new trilby.

"If you've got a hat on you can raise it, doff it, greet with it. What I'd like to get going is a campaign of courtesy though not for its own sake. I believe that such courtesy and politeness is demanded of us as Christians in order that we might acknowledge each other's worth as children of God.

"Will you please join me in a campaign of courtesy? Remember, the politeness and consideration we would be advocating and practising would not just be in order to make the world a pleasant and more agreeable place to live in, but because it is demanded of us that we acknowledge and affirm each other as a brother or a sister for whom Christ died."

Donald Gray,
Canon of Westminster, Rector of St Margaret's &
Chaplain to the Speaker of the House of Commons

Chapter Four

MANNERS NOW?

By Duff Hart-Davis, reprinted with permission from

The Sunday Telegraph

Are we degenerating into a nation of boors, brutalised by the pressures of a highly competitive existence? And if we are, does it matter?

A random survey shows that manners are in decline, and that many people are dismayed by the trend.

It would be unreasonable to expect that manners should remain static: they are bound to change with the times. But the way in which manners are observed or disregarded affects everybody.

The question is: what sort of behaviour is appropriate or acceptable now? What role do manners play in modern society?

As most people perceive them, manners are the little courtesies that minimise friction between human beings. Often they are confused with etiquette: it is hard to lay down where one ends and the other begins. To say "please" and "thank you" is obviously good manners – but the way you hold your knife at table is more a matter of etiquette.

Clearly the elaborate etiquette of Victorian and Edwardian days is obsolete; but as life becomes more hectic and society more crowded, the need for considerate behaviour would seem to be greater than ever. Nevertheless, among young people a thoroughly relaxed code of conduct prevails.

This casual attitude is often attributed to the Welfare State. "Young people get given so much that they take everything for granted," said one business executive. "If a boy is awarded an educational grant or a scholarship, it doesn't occur to him to say thank you to the authorities. He just thinks it's his right – and this attitude spreads into personal relationships."

At least two major companies – Lloyds Bank and W.H. Smith – are running extensive and expensive training schemes to improve their staff's behaviour. "There has certainly been a decline in the standard of manners over the past two years, in every respect," says Don Porter, Lloyds' Chief Manager, Corporate Communications, who was brought into the firm from British Airways to effect a transformation. "We don't say we're disastrously bad, but we're looking for that notch up that will put us ahead of competitors."

To this end Mr Porter has launched his "Customer First" programme. By next February every member of Lloyds' 54,000 staff in the UK will have gone through a one-day "customer workshop," which includes sessions on manners, good and bad service, and how to treat customers generally. Particular attention is given to body language and to "strokes" – an American name for compliments.

"Customers like to have their egos pampered," says Mr Porter. "What we're teaching is really the old, traditional good manners in a new package. We're re-stating the common courtesies."

To keep their attention focused in the right direction, staff in all the bank's branches now have blockpads of scribbling paper inscribed with "Customer First" slogans: "Make their day . . . A smile can be heard on the phone . . . First impressions last . . . Good manners cost nothing but are worth a great deal."

At W.H. Smith there has been a similar realisation that uncouth staff turn customers off and away. "First Service," aimed initially at the firm's 13,000 retail staff, is described as an "attitudinal training" programme. "Courtesy is very much part of it," says Mrs Sheila Hughes, the executive in charge. "The most important thread running through it is that you can do an awful lot of harm by bad manners, and undo an awful lot by good manners."

Here, too, staff are taught to use and exploit body-language. In one exercise each member of a group is given a card with an emotion written on it – frustration, irritation, impatience, satisfaction – and asked to portray that feeling without words. In another, as one person is telling a story, the rest deliberately stop listening, to let him or her find out how annoying that can be.

According to Mrs Hughes, people are so fascinated by examining their own behaviour that "the scheme has put a buzz around the whole company." Whether coincidentally or not, the number of customer complaints has dropped substantially since "First Service" was introduced.

At both W.H. Smith and Lloyds it is perceived that the fall-off in manners is closely linked to a decline in standards of literacy. Simon Hornby, Smith's chief executive, has launched a drive to raise standards, recognising that someone not confident about reading and writing in general is simply not able to compose a good business letter, let alone a thank-you one.

One development that has unsettled many boys is the advance of feminism. A young American on his first visit to London was amazed when, standing up on a crowded tube train and offering his seat to a woman, he was blasted by a yell of "SEXIST!" This kind of thing has made many young men nervous about extending traditional courtesies, for fear of being abused or ridiculed. At the same time, it is equally clear that non-militant females do still appreciate being looked after.

An unofficial poll, conducted for The Sunday Telegraph among the 50 girls at Evendine Court, the finishing school near Malvern, revealed that all of them like having doors opened and expect boys to stand up when they come into a room. Further, although they enjoy such attention themselves, they consider it much more important that it should be extended to adults.

Although they admit that in private their own manners are slovenly and that they eat like pigs whenever there is no need to put on a show, they do lift standards in more formal surroundings. Altogether their Principal, Rosamund Trafford-Roberts, describes their attitudes as "amazingly old-fashioned."

Teenage boys and young men also tend to behave like chameleons. In private they are Belloc's ruffians,

> Who take their manners from the Ape,
> Their habits from the Bear.

But on more formal occasions they come up neat, polished and smiling. Equally, in the office, although they may favour designer jeans and stubble for everyday wear, they appear clean-shaven and in a suit if they know they are going to have lunch with the boss.

Some observers believe that the changes have been so profound as to alienate one generation from the next – and certainly one of the most painful things is to hear children insulting their parents. I came across one family in which the behaviour of teenage children became so obnoxious that in the end their father was driven out of his home.

All day they lounged about the place dressed in towels, watching his television, drinking his drink, eating his food and, whenever he appeared, abusing him in obscene terms. The only way he could get rid of them was to sell the house and move into a flat too small to accommodate them.

Some people tend to equate behaviour with matters

of class; but others claim that class makes little difference, and that good or bad manners please or rankle at any level of society. Thus Mrs Trafford-Roberts is determined that her girls should behave consistently, no matter whom they are with: "I should be furious if I found that they had treated a member of the domestic staff less courteously than they would treat me."

Again, Bob and Liz, the couple who run our village shop, and who would be the first to describe themselves as ordinary country people, have such good manners that a visit to their establishment is always a pleasure. A notice on the counter, copied from a local school, proclaims: "Unlike boots and shoes, the words please and thank you never wear out. Use them as often as you like." And Bob, I am glad to hear, gives a salutary dressing-down to any nipper who fails to take heed of the invitation.

Even if standards in general have fallen, there still exist bastions of traditional manners, not least the public schools. At Winchester, for instance, the motto "Manners Makyth Man" is upheld as keenly today as when it was coined nearly six centuries ago. In the view of Lord Aldington, who for the past eight years has been Warden, or titular head, of the College, the boys are admirably behaved.

Michael Marland, headmaster of North Westminster Community School, a large comprehensive in Paddington, believes that, far from there being a decline, "the general level of young people's courtesy has been going up over the past ten years. I guarantee that if I were to walk into my Upper School now, the pupils coming out of morning class would turn and smile and say, 'Hello, Sir'– whereas when I was at school and saw the headmaster coming, we used to look the other way."

Mr Marland attributes this happy state of affairs partly to the fact that his school has a good disciplinary structure, "so that the adults can be courteous and aren't always shouting at the children, most of whom will be courteous in return."

Another strong influence is the wide range of ethnic backgrounds from which his pupils are drawn. "A mixture like this makes you think more about other people. If your best friend's first language is Amharic, and your next best friend is English, you can't take other people for granted."

Comparison with foreigners can be instructive. Indians, for instance, often strike me as having perfect natural manners – but this is probably because they have been brought up strictly by their parents.

"In my country the family, and religion, are still much stronger than here," says Prafulla Mohanti, an author and artist who came to England nearly 30 years ago. "From their earliest years children are taught to respect their parents, their elders, and above all strangers – for who knows? God may arrive in the guise of a stranger, to test you. So Indian people tend to be much more hospitable."

Mr Mohanti – himself the gentlest of men – finds English people growing more and more selfish. "I'm amazed by how aggressive everyone is. Aggression is appreciated much more than gentleness, which is seen as weakness. But my mother's strength was her gentleness."

This is the nub of the matter: taking trouble with one's fellow human beings. For the fact that not enough trouble is now taken, most people blame parents first, schools second.

What can be done? Perhaps a national drive is needed. One of my informants asked me why television should not be used to teach manners – a good question, since, as this person pointed out, most comedy programmes consist exclusively of the characters swapping insults. The subject is certainly of national importance, for as that acute observer, the Duchess of Devonshire, pointed out, "manners are what oil the wheels of life," and without them life becomes uncomfortably abrasive.

Chapter Five

THE SINGAPORE EXPERIENCE

The Government of Singapore has mounted a "national courtesy campaign" every year since 1979, under the conviction that good inter-personal relations between people in a crowded environment are of the greatest importance.

The Government puts an umbrella budget of approaching £200,000 into the campaign, and major companies are pleased to be associated with it in the form of sponsorship for specific projects.

The campaign lasts throughout the year, but July is "courtesy month" with an intensive mass-media public communication programme. It has without doubt helped Singapore to avoid a good many of the social and communal problems which you might expect in a multi-race highly competitive society.

When Prime Minister Lee Kuan Yew launched the campaign in 1979 he recalled that it started when the Singapore Tourist Board wanted to encourage people to be more polite to tourists. But it came to have a wider significance.

"We must teach children and persuade adults to be courteous to each other," he said.

"We want to be courteous because life will be better for all. Courtesy is part of all cultivated societies. It is a desirable attitude in itself. To be courteous to free–spending tourists and rude to fellow Singaporeans is to demean ourselves. Then we become a despicable people, moved only by thought of profit."

The Prime Minister noted that four different languages were spoken in his country, with many different dialects, but in them all the true language of courtesy was sincerity.

"Behind the words and gestures there must be sincere consideration for the other person's right to self-respect, self-esteem and well-being. Polite people put others at ease because they treat others with respect as fellow human beings.

"Courtesy begets courtesy: discourtesy provokes discourtesy," he went on. Mr Lee said good manners usually resulted from good breeding. It was hard for people to be courteous to each other when they were struggling for bare survival. Whatever courtesy refugees had practised in Cambodia or Vietnam vanished under the pressure to get enough space, food and attention in order to survive. But every society that achieved more than a bare subsistence acquired a minimal cultural gloss for their inter-personal relationships.

Societies that had achieved sustained prosperity often evolved elaborate forms of social civility, especially at the capital, the centre of their civilisation.

He recalled that Singapore had passed through "a riotous and anxious phase" in the 1950s, and had overcome the difficulties. "We became a rugged society in the 1960s. Then with unemployment and uncertainties overcome we created a pleasant physical environment, a clean and green city in the 1970s." The campaign in the 1980s was to create a pleasant social environment with Singaporeans considerate to each other and thoughtful of each other's needs.

Children must be taught better manners at home and school. "We can succeed," said the Prime Minister. "We are better fed, dressed and housed. Living in high rise new towns, working in high rise offices and factories, travelling in crowded buses and lifts, our lives will be unbearable if we are all selfish and inconsiderate.

"Greater courtesy will help us to be psychologically better adjusted, with less pent-up frustrations. If we set our minds on it we can be a better-mannered society."

The campaign began in earnest, with a theme for each year. "Make courtesy our way of life" was the theme in 1979. The emphasis was on civil service, with a need for a review of regulations and office layout to provide efficiency and courtesy to callers. The objective was to motivate government departments and private organisations to take courtesy seriously.

In the following year the objective was to emphasise the need for courtesy between colleagues and neighbours. Subsequent years have aimed at improving relationships between management and workers, and the importance of courtesy in daily living. A courtesy mascot, "Singa", was introduced in 1982. Social responsibility was the theme for 1983, and in the following year people were reminded that courtesy was in them, and it should be demonstrated. "A little thought means so much" was the thought behind the 1985 and 1986 campaigns, and in 1987 an ambitious programme of events was launched in "Singa City" with "a month of courtesy that will last a lifetime."

The advertising ran: " . . . Here, kids can learn courtesy in fun-filled ways while adults enjoy the lavish displays of an atrium transformed into a little theme park.

"Our exciting programme includes variety shows, workshops, skits, the Great Courtesy Quest where you make your way through fun-filled courtesy stations and are rewarded with an attractive souvenir, a courtesy drive where shoppers 'caught' being courteous by a mystery spotter win prizes, a telephone courtesy contest, computer games and other exciting happenings . . . customers at some stores would receive courtesy T shirts. So come to Singa City, where courtesy has never been this much fun!"

The event attracted 941,000 visitors – about three times the number expected, and 80 schools took some 7,000 students to see and take part in it. More than 200 people were rewarded for courteous and considerate acts. The event cost £100,000 and was aimed at getting over the message that courtesy is a way of life. Young people's organisations like Girl Guides, Scouts and the Boys' Brigade sent 1,800 volunteers to man booths, and there were workshops on such things as table manners and body language which were well attended.

The National University of Singapore held a four-day live-in seminar for 200 pre-university and junior college students on courtesy. Some 2,000 T-shirts and 3,000 balloons with the Youth Challenge courtesy logo were on offer for sale.

The courtesy campaign in Singapore proceeds with enthusiasm, sniped at from time to time by acerbic western journalists who sneer at "the politeness police" and the "courtesy cops", suggesting that people should be allowed the human freedom of being discourteous if they wish.

Mr Lee Kwan Yew, however, persists with the philosophy behind the drive. In 1980 he said that societies could turn sour. "When I went to Britain as a student in 1946, I found a people courteous and gracious, despite six years of war, destruction and deprivation. London was then the centre of a great civilisation, justly proud of its role in the last war and conscious that it was a centre of great decisions and events which affected the world.

"Over the last three decades, returning for periodic visits, I watched with sadness a gradual roughening of inter-personal relationships. The British economy was overtaken by that of the other EEC countries, especially Germany and France.

"The British people lost heart, watching successive

governments unable to reverse the trend of events. British management became demoralised by endless squabbles with intransigent trade union leaders re-fighting old battles. Their self-esteem was shaken, so they lost that glow of graciousness which only a self-confident people can exude. British drivers, once the most considerate and courteous, have became as aggressive as those in Europe, though not as bad as ours.

"Courtesies have become perfunctory; personal standards of honesty have gone down. Vandalism in trains, football stadia and other public places, unheard of 30 years ago, have become part of contemporary Britain."

Mr Lee said no society was static. The world moved on and every society went up or down. He hoped that by 1990 in Singapore they could file down the rough ragged corners of social behaviour which could grate on each other. "Politeness can reflect genuine consideration for each other's dignity and well-being: it is part of a well-ordered society determined to improve the social as well as the material aspects of life."

But he warned that money could not buy courtesy, which was "one manifestation of civilised living, the result of attention to the finer points of human relationships over many years . . . By persistent effort our children can grow up naturally polite: they should not need courtesy campaigns."

By the second year of the campaign, the Prime Minister was claiming that there had been progress.

"Telephone operators and counter clerks in the Government offices have improved. Taxi drivers and bus conductors are more polite. There have been fewer complaints of rudeness. Service in hotels and restaurants is more courteous."

Many bad habits remained, all the same. Motorists were impatient and inconsiderate. In eating places, shops and some large department stores servers and sales girls were inattentive and indifferent. Courtesy taught in schools was being undone by the rude behaviour students met outside school.

Mr Lee said they had achieved easier targets like checking vandals and litter droppers. Those could be punished. "But we cannot punish people because they refuse to smile or be pleasant. It is much more difficult to induce good behaviour. Courtesy and good human relations spring from a genuine respect for each other as fellow citizens."

He thought it would be a decade before they were rid of unpleasant habits of inconsiderate, selfish behaviour. "As a young society of migrant stock we have tended to be self-centred and to be helpful and charitable only within the family, and at a pinch within the extended clan. To raise our level of social achievement we have to extend a part of the respect and consideration we have for members of our family to our neighbours and our fellow workers."

Students of human nature may be sceptical, but there is no doubting the determination of this administration to achieve a social revolution rarely attempted in human history. Mr Lee looked in this speech for "incremental improvements in our human relations each year." If they could do it, within ten years those who were not by nature considerate would find themselves surrounded by considerate people "who, through social pressure, will shame the errant minority into behaving considerately."

He insisted that it could be done. "An executive who is polite to his subordinates in the office or in the factory is also a polite motorist. Because he is polite he evokes politeness from his secretaries and his workers and from fellow drivers on the roads.

"The objective is to create a total environment in which courteous, considerate and co-operative behaviour becomes a way of life."

In the following year, 1982, Premier Lee noted the attitude of the Japanese, who were amongst the most polite of people, although they had some of the world's most densely populated cities. They also had the highest productivity. The Germans, also polite and formal, had high productivity. One lesson to learn from other people was that no society was guaranteed a position at the top of the league as the most polite and productive. "People change: they grow older. The next generation is never the same. They may be as good or better: they may degenerate and be worse."

He said they had been able to change Singapore with its dirty smelly streets and drains choked with rubbish, and rivers stinking with garbage, into a clean and green city. It had been possible because of their receptivity to new ideas, and being open to reason and logic.

"The easier changes have been achieved: anti-vandalism, anti-littering by better policing, better public cleansing, and better maintenance. The more difficult targets are higher education, better work attitudes, and more considerate and co-operative conduct."

A more detailed analysis of social problems in Singapore was attempted by Mr S. Rajaratnam, second deputy prime minister, when he opened the 1983 campaign. They had an immigrant community and all Singapore people originated from rich and complex civilisations well known for their graceful manners and courteous conduct.

It may be that when people came to Singapore they brought with them all sorts of rituals and superstitions "but left behind the graceful ways and considerate conduct."

He thought one reason for the low priority of courtesy was the average man's "single-minded devotion to moneytheism. His ancestors came to Singapore to make money, not learn manners. Courtesy was something that could not be quantified and for some Singaporeans anything that could not be quantified was not worth the acquisition."

Mr Rajaratnam did not believe that material success and courteous behaviour were incompatible. The Japanese had proved that. "In fact it is my impression that bad manners and economic and political backwardness go together; that high standards of courtesy have gone hand in hand with high civilisation."

He quoted Professor Norbert Elias, a Swiss sociologist, who in a two volume work examined the relationship between courteous conduct and the advance of civilisation, and Mr Rajaratnam concluded: "It is unnatural for large groups of men to live together in close proximity. Unless we devise rules and regulations to smooth out the stress and strains of mass society we will, as has happened in many countries, transform a city into a jungle where men become uncouth barbarians."

The fledgling British Polite Society could not say better what its foundation principles are than in words used by Mr Goh Chok Tong, First Deputy Prime Minister, when he launched the Singapore campaign in 1985. He looked forward to 1999 and asked whether his country could be richer in material things then and at the same time be gracious, refined, and cultured. "Will striving for higher standards of living make us think only of ourselves or give thought also to others? Will owning our own homes make us feel more secure or more smug and selfish?"

It is interesting to hear an emerging society articulate these questions, for they are just the questions we must ask ourselves in the newly prosperous United Kingdom. Mr Goh thought people could be materially as well as spiritually better off if they set their minds to it, and he underlined the critical importance of what we affirm in the Polite Society when he added: "The starting point is courtesy."

He went on: "Courtesy is a matter for the home, the neighbourhood, the school and the workplace. Let us work together for a total environment of courtesy.

"How you sound on the telephone, the expressions you use in your letter, the look on your face and the tone of your voice when you serve the public across the counter, all very quickly indicate whether you believe in courtesy or not. It is not just a matter of words: one can detect hypocrisy even if the words 'please' and 'thank you' are used. A shopkeeper who is rude to his customers will quickly change when his customers stop coming. A civil servant who is rude to the public adds one more dent to the whole image of the Government."

He said he would like to see special awards to courteous people in the retail, transport and public service areas, and concluded: "The goal of a gracious and pleasant society is a worthwhile one for all of us. It is part of a society of distinction. We can make Singapore such a society if we all pitch in. We either determine the values for society or we drift along without values. Let us resolve to be a courteous society."

After a ten year campaign, how has life in Singapore been affected? There is no doubt about the thoroughness with which it has been tackled and the enthusiasm of commercial organisations in coming forward as sponsors. Training programmes, leaflets, posters, window stickers, balloons, a video, a pop song, and all the razzmatazz of show business has been brought into play. In 1988 a leading Japanese company expressed interest in sponsoring the campaign. We asked a Government spokesman to sum up how effective it had all been in terms of bringing up children, industrial productivity and the behaviour of people in sporting events. This was the reply:

"The Courtesy Campaign plays a very important and effective role in industrial productivity, sporting events and in terms of helping parents and teachers in bringing up children. Parents are reminded of the part they play as 'role models' for their children to emulate and I am glad to say, many are aware of this even without the ministry's constant reminders through campaign messages. In schools the teachers play an important role in leadership by example. Courtesy is also taught to students as part of the moral education programme.

"There is no denying that courtesy is an effective medium in promoting industrial productivity. Courtesy is seen as a social glue promoting social cohesion, less stress at the work place, teamwork and ultimately productivity. Working together as a team, workers are able to work in harmony and produce better results for their respective organisations and ultimately the nation.

"With regard to courtesy's effect on the behaviour of people at sporting events, Singaporeans are usually well-behaved, either as participants or members of the audience. However, we do recognise the need for sporting enthusiasts to be also reminded of the need for courtesy. The public behaviour of certain opinion leaders, leading sporting personalities and stars are considered acceptable behaviour. Therefore the 'shaping' of the personality of people in sporting events will definitely need such personalities to take the lead."

The Straits Times interpreted the slogan for 1987: Courtesy: it begins with me as a call for people to make the first friendly move to other people in their daily dealings. They should initiate goodwill rather than react to it. The writer looked back over the years and found that "every imaginable means of gently persuading people to be more conscious of good manners has been tried. The question to ask today is "Are we anywhere near the kind of society that Mr Lee envisaged in 1981? What else must we do?" Most of the 50 people the paper interviewed said rudeness was on the decline. People had become more mindful of the need to be courteous, but they doubted whether Singaporeans had reached the stage where courtesy came naturally. A conscious effort was being made by many to demonstrate good manners and tolerance.

A booklet issued by the Singapore Ministry of Communications and Information asks, "What is courtesy?" and answers thus:

"Courtesy is being considerate of others' feelings. It is thinking before we act. If we take time to think how our words and actions affect others, there will be fewer opportunities of hurting others unintentionally. We will treat others the way we would like to be treated.

"Courtesy is respect for our elders and our family members. It is also respect for other people's way of life and for communal and public property. Courtesy is being helpful to people you know and to people you don't know. It is being responsive to people in need, like helping in the community, and in charity, and in covering your colleague's duties in his/her absence.

"Courtesy is being polite to all people, not only to our family and friends, but also to total strangers as well. It begins with ourselves. So often we wait for others to make the first move. Why not be the first to start?"

Mrs Jean Barratt Patton, a Polite Society member of Bloomington, Indiana, USA, sent a copy of her local paper with the following advert:
"My apologies to the funeral procession going west on third street through Highland Village for driving through the procession . . ."

Mrs Patton writes:

"The American tourist is apparently unloved because of a failure to conform to British ways, but how is he to know what they are? If only we could work out, and establish, the Anglo-American Code of Proprieties perhaps we could jointly stand firm against the attacks of the various other societies."

Chapter Six

COURTESY IN CONTEXT

by Patricia M.Wharton

What do we mean by politeness or good manners today? Ideals of good social behaviour have varied greatly between different times, places, communities and classes. Some modern sociologists would doubtless regard such ideals as purely relative and of no permanent significance. In recent years even some moralists and theologians have tended to favour what are called "situational" ethics.

Yet, if our generally acceptable standards are to vary so widely, according to individual requirements, it is very hard to see how any particular rules of politeness can be devised or applied. Again, if there is no generally recognised agreement or consensus in society about fundamental morality, it is only too easy for alienated people to represent particular manners as merely class-based snobbish conventions, of purely fashionable or ephemeral interest. Thus, many egalitarians, radicals and anarchists have been moved to protest by adopting Bohemian lifestyles and speech, often deliberately designed to offend those whom they consider but selfish hypocrites.

There is now, for instance, no generally accepted image of the good man, let alone the good woman; the old ideals of lady and gentleman seem hopelessly dated. In an increasingly egalitarian age, indeed, is there a place for such ideals? Members of The Polite Society may not yet realise how difficult are the questions they are posing and how far they may have to seek for satisfactory answers.

Many Christians, losing patience with all this, may wish to simplify the whole problem by emphasising the Golden Rule of Benevolence or consideration for others and those of other religions may have very similar charitable principles. Indeed, the extent of cultural relativism in the field of basic morals may perhaps be greatly exaggerated, since most societies find it necessary to legislate against murder, theft etc. and some of the most "primitive" may have the very strongest social sanctions. It is usually only in detribalised societies or urban jungles that the need for any such rules is denied. Yet, as to the details of good manners societies do vary greatly.

The precise connections between kindness and politeness on the one hand and cruelty and rudeness on the other are more complicated than at first appear. Some of the cruellest people in history have also been icily polite, while, in contrast, some of the kindest of men have been famous for their rudeness or asperity. So, in the past, there have been many formally polite societies which yet practised terrible cruelties; feudal China and Japan and Medieval Europe come to mind.

Duellists offered each other elaborate bows and salutes before engaging in mortal combat and executioners begged forgiveness of their victims before dismembering or disembowelling them! Such paradoxes are expressed also in literature, where Satan, who, according to Dante, lived in the deepest pit of Hell which was not hot but icily cold, is most often depicted as a beautiful charmer, a cool and callous con-man in fact. People who met Hitler also remarked on his "charm".

In sharpest contrast, such varied humanitarians as Dr Johnson, Dean Swift and Voltaire abhorred sentimentality and loved to pose as misanthropists. Thus, Dr Johnson, the Tory High Churchman with an acidic wit, was so compassionate that he took unfortunates into his own house to share his simple fare, while Dean Swift, who wrote the most unforgiving satires on the rich and powerful, yet was so distressed by the poverty he encountered in Ireland that he abounded in personal abnegation and works of charity. As for Voltaire, Diderot wrote to his mistress Sophie Volland a charming fable about his famous friend: "Someone gives him a shocking page which Rousseau, citizen of Geneva, has just scribbled against him. He gets furious, he loses his temper, he calls him villain, he foams with rage; he wants to have the miserable fellow beaten to death. 'Look,' says someone there. 'I have it on good authority that he's going to ask you for asylum, today, tomorrow, perhaps the day after tomorrow. What would you do?' . . . 'What would I do?' replies Voltaire, gnashing his teeth. 'What would

I do? I'd take him by the hand, lead him to my room, and say to him: "Look, here's my bed, the best in the house, sleep there – sleep there for the rest of your life, and be happy".' [Vol. 1 p.5 *The Enlightenment* by Peter Gay].

Likewise, the ancient Hebrew prophets were past masters of invective and abuse. No anti-semite ever castigated the children of Israel as harshly for their failings as Jeremiah and all the rest, but of course one has to look at their motivation. Their anger was impelled by love of God and concern that his people should obey his commandments. Christ himself continued in the same prophetic tradition, losing his temper with the money changers and abusing the Pharisees as hypocrites in the same earthy language, while his remarks to the Samaritan woman, likening her people to dogs, would have got him into trouble with the modern day race relations industry. But of course he was a poet too, and poets, like comics, must be allowed the licence of strong language. There seems then to be a place for righteous indignation and even for righteous rudeness, as Bob Geldof's recent outbursts against the complacency of various politicians and bureaucrats have also illustrated. Yet also, to be effective, such anger and strong language must be reserved for the really appropriate occasion; if they become the norm they lose their capacity for good and become evil.

The reformer very often stands out on account of his contrariness. In times of peace and prosperity society is inclined to become over-civilised and refined, complacent, and conventional. Both art and etiquette become dessicated and "mannered". Dead customs may persist as barren rituals, degenerating into compulsive and obsessional ceremonies like the Japanese tea ritual. In these circumstances, the reformer, setting out to shock, may perform a useful service in puncturing pomposity with wit and irony, like the original plain Quakers refusing to doff their hats. Yet we must remember that all these customs had originally some valid purpose which was doubtless to smoothe and facilitate social meetings, in much the same way as routine in work, or rules of play, are useful in preventing friction and fatigue.

In contrast, therefore, the reformer, in times of anarchy and violence, when all civilised standards seem to have broken down may set out to surprise, if not to shock, by the punctilious observance of good manners. Thus the writer Laurens van der Post describes in one novel how he saved his life during the last war by greeting his Japanese captors civilly in their own language. Then in 1987, Penelope Tremayne, aged 65, and travelling alone in Sri Lanka, survived capture by Tamil Tiger guerrillas because she refused either to fear her captors or to berate them. Dickens in "The Tale of Two Cities"[1], describes how, during the French Revolution, the only places where conventional good manners could still be found were the prisons, full of condemned aristocrats. Yet it is not only at the top of society or in extreme circumstances that people find the time and inclination for elaborate etiquette. Poor and simple but leisurely societies often develop complex forms of address, while it has been observed that the Jews of the Russian ghettos cultivated an extreme politeness and concern for each others' feelings, seemingly to compensate for the persecutions and pogroms without. [2]

Viewed in historical perspective, however, we can perceive successive and alternating periods in the general history of behaviour. To take well-known examples from Roman history, we find that in a small city state the way of life and manners tended to be simple and sincere, as befitting a peasant people still retaining strong links with the lan. The Romans themselves valued this "gravitas". Success, conquest and expansion brought prosperity and improved standards of living, higher levels of culture and Greek schoolmasters. But such growth also led to an influx of slaves and class conflict between patricians and plebeans. So, at the height of Roman power, we find a plutocracy of big landowners, merchants and wealthy senators replacing the old and virile warrior aristocracy, with mercenaries brought in to make up for the lack of native Roman soldiers. The upper class becomes increasingly corrupt and decadent, indulging in every vice, luxury, and gluttony and enjoying cruel public games. Emperors are often murdered and succeed each other in rapid succession, relying on the support of their guards rather than any popular mandate. Only the army and the civil service provide some continuity. Finally, in her declining years, Rome, like a wicked and ageing empress, is assailed by greedy predators – dissidents from within and barbarians from without, until the whole decaying edifice crumbles and falls.

In the ensuing Dark Ages of chaos and civil strife, all civilised ways and manners also disappeared for a time, since all that counted was the barest survival. Yet gradually, with the aid of the Christian Church, even out of all this anarchy, a new civilisation grew up, that of the Middle Ages, with Medieval Europe conceived of as united Christendom.

Turning now from this general European history to the case of our own country, or, "The Matter of Britain", how can we consider changing customs in their historical context? Most of our expressions for good manners are of French origin, e.g. chivalry, courtesy, politeness, and etiquette. This suggests that it was the Norman conquerors and their royal and aristocratic successors who first introduced and appreciated the finer points of social behaviour. Yet that would not be altogether fair on their predecessors.

The Ancient Celts, Anglo Saxons and Danes certainly had a simpler and more basic lifestyle, but they were by no means uncivilised. Their favourite stories may well be apocryphal, but in each case they illustrate a social ideal – that of Arthur, "the once and future king" and his knights of the Round Table, who battled against the invading pagan Saxons; and then of Alfred, the Anglo-Saxon champion against the Danes, who was simple and modest in his social relations and not afraid to rough it. Finally there was Canute, the Danish Christian king, who exposed the pretensions of his court flatterers by humbly revealing his own human limitations. Courage, chivalry, dedication and humility were to become the classic aspirations of the Christian gentleman.

The psychological value of a king or queen may well be that of representing an ideal type for the ordinary man or woman to emulate and the worth of a royal family is correspondingly greater still. Commissars, politicians, film and pop stars, even Presidents of Republics, seldom perform this function so well. Ever since the legendary and numinous King Arthur, the monarch has been "hedged with divinity", but at the same time our wisest rulers have always understood the need to retain the common touch and to counteract the corrupting effects of political power by training their heirs to rough it. So, even today, members of the royal family regularly take physical risks which most of us softies would hesitate to undertake.

The early warrior aristocracy is also now shrouded for us in a certain heroic legend, although, in reality, it was only but partially civilised. Yet the great lords liked to imagine the ideal knight and his lady as also paragons of courage, chivalry, dedication and humility, so that, in course of time, noblemen too were expected to set a good example of "noblesse oblige", by their services to the state and to charity. Yet just as aristocracies could once easily revert to cruel and arrogant robber barons, later they could grow into greedy, plutocratic élites and in either case offend more basic egalitarian sentiments. So, from time to time, there is always a call for greater simplicity, sincerity and democracy and the reform of over-elaborate social customs and manners which appear, like the sumptuary restrictions on the wearing of certain clothes and ornaments, merely to buttress social divisions.

Moreover, for all this time, some more private and personal ideals of good conduct also developed, although these were still highly dependent on one's status in a hierarchical society. Thus the honest medieval townsman had to make do with tales of that original yuppie, the ingenious and self-made burgher, Dick Whittington, and the peasant with the rustic tales of Robin Hood, to express his needs for social justice, equality and carefree fellowship.

Therefore, in the course of English history we can trace, not so much as for Rome, a once and for all curve of rise and fall, as a sequence of periods alternately conservative and revolutionary, with perhaps some transitional times in between. One sharp contrast in manners which springs to mind, is that between the Puritan period and the Restoration. The Puritans affected a simplicity and plainness in religion, dress, and speech and gravity of demeanour which eschewed frivolity, music, dancing and plays, but they gained unpopularity for their joyless bigotry and hypocrisy. So, with the Restoration, high society enjoyed a permissive age of drinking, gambling, wenching and bawdy comedies. But, in time, this too degenerated into self-indulgence and decadence, until the very word "cavalier" came to signify, not so much "gay and charming", as "selfish and off-hand".

Yet, with the passing of the Stuarts, the monarchy and the court lost an essential charisma and mystique. Thus, Queen Anne was the last monarch to touch (or lay on hands) people for the cure of diseases. Only in our own day, has Princess Diana, herself of Stuart descent, recovered this quality. So, in the eighteenth century, the dull and unpopular Georges could no longer say, like Henry V to his future queen, "We are the makers of manners, Kate". [Shakespeare]

Instead it was left largely to the newly entrenched Whig aristocracy to set the tone for high society. Indeed they presided over an age of unparalleled elegance in architecture, furnishing and landscape-gardening, and they collected books and objets d'art from their continental grand tours. At this level of society social relations also became more refined and the great town and country houses in and around London, Bath, Brighton and other resorts, became the setting for all the balls, dinners and parties demanded by this "polite society", as described in the novels of Jane Austen.

However, the late 18th century also witnessed the coming of the agrarian and industrial revolutions and the crowding of an increasing population into the "dark satanic mills" and new industrial towns of the north. Class divisions were exacerbated and most of the new factory owners did not have the paternalistic feelings towards their work-people that the best of the old landowners had for their tenants and dependents. To make matters worse, the humanitarian reformers and societies which had begun to get going in this "Age of Reason", were soon discouraged by the reaction to the French Revolution. This had been welcomed at first in England, but later feared and hated because of the Terror and the revolutionary wars to which it led.

When the wars and the long reaction were over, it was left largely to the middle classes to set the new social ideals of the 19th century industrial age, and it was they who modified the old ideal of the gentleman, to include not only the traditional squires, but also the newly respectable merchants and manufacturers. They were fortunate in having, as their royal and social figure-heads, a quintessentially bourgeois couple in Queen Victoria and Prince Albert, who shared the same concerns for family and industry.

Meanwhile, this new concept of gentility, as an ideal to which all could eventually aspire, was even extended by some to include, in time, also "nature's gentlemen" among the respectable yeomen and artisans. Yet it is not surprising that the new ideal of the "gentleman" did not appeal to all. It had shrunk somehow, from the concept of the chivalrous knight – still commemorated in the suffix esquire – to the bourgeois ideal of the merely respectable or prudent citizen, sometimes indeed the false "bonhomme", serious hard-working, thrifty and temperate even, but never again so dashing, gallant, generous or charming as the best of cavaliers.

After all, there had long been social protests. Both before and after the Peasants Revolt and the Lollard, minstrels sang, "When Adam delved and Eve span who was then the gentleman?" affirming the ideal of a simpler and more democratic fraternity. Much later, the new French Republic, inspired by the Quaker, Thomas Paine, had declared "The Rights of Man" and the brotherhood of all Republican citizens, principles which, of course, were soon violated, as in all other revolutions, by the atrocities of the Terror. Yet the earliest British Socialists, undeterred, took up the cry for equality and fraternity and for economic as well as political liberty. Robert Owen developed his model factory system, and also advocated the formation of ideal communities, co-operatives and trade unions. His successors also promoted welfare and mutual aid and, the more to emphasise equality, called each other "brother" or "comrade". Similar terms are the Australian "mate" and the West Indian "man". By the end of the 19th century several of the Chartists' points of political reform had been gained, but more economic equality was as far away as ever.

So the British class system remained virtually intact until the Great War, in spite of such protests from organised Labour, and also from women and from the Irish, Scots and Welsh on the fringes of Britain who still felt excluded from power in the mainstream society, although Lloyd George emerged and pushed his way to the top and, later on, Ramsay Macdonald. It was the tragic war itself and its mismanagement that led to really widespread disillusion with the values and institutions of both the residual aristocratic leadership and the middle class morality. This conflict which killed off some of the very best young men and left their womenfolk freer, but also lonelier, than ever before, produced a deep cynicism and despair, particularly on the Continent. Countries appeared to recover for a time, but then the economic depression set in, and political opinions became increasingly polarised between socialists, who now took Soviet Communism as their ideal, and conservatives, more and more tempted into reaction, or to timid emulation or appeasement of the fascist powers. It was no accident that the liberal parties declined everywhere; moderation, tolerance and urbanity were no longer admired.

The only new ideals of manhood (and womanhood) were more basic and brutal, not to say barbarian. Hitler admired the German superman, who was not conceived as a mature, well-rounded man, but rather as a permanent juvenile delinquent, the callow blonde beast a perfect mate for Hollywood's ideal dumb blonde. While Stalin, we now know, favoured only yes-men and faceless bureaucrats to carry out his commands, as he slaughtered his old revolutionary comrades.

In this new harsh climate of opinion, the rights of men and women were increasingly disregarded for reasons of party, state or nationality, and humanitarianism, often called vaguely "democracy", "Christianity" or even "socialism", came to be seen as a weak and sentimental ideology and a symptom of decadence in the West. The great crusading humanitarian reformers of the 19th century, with their heroic sense of duty and formidable capacity for service and self-sacrifice, were conveniently forgotten.

Nevertheless, in an England insulated still from

many sad Continental influences, some urbanity survived, together with a native moderation and what G.K. Chesterton has so well described as "a love of English cosiness". Even in the very depressed areas, crime and delinquency rates were still low by modern standards, for sense of grievance very rarely matches reality of grievance, and working people still helped each other in the spirit of Methodism, or co-operation, mutual-aid and utopian (i.e. humanitarian) socialism. Meanwhile, the middle classes maintained a genteel respectability and even the upper classes adjusted themselves stoically to ever heavier taxation. Great efforts were made to keep the peace, welfare measures were improved and the thirties witnessed a modest economic recovery and higher living standards.

The Second World War shattered this calm and again strained the country, but there was less loss of young men and the great effort united the various classes as never before in a common struggle and led to greater equality, e.g. through food rationing. The spirit of the blitz and of the Battle of Britain was one of renewed consensus and, in many ways, of renewed hope.

Wartime austerities continued into the fifties and were more and more resented, but the Labour government did lay the foundations for the Welfare State, on the basis of a consensus which has only very recently been questioned. The old class system was still further weakened and, in the permissive sixties, the flood-gates of social mobility were opened, and working class popstars qualified for M.B.E.s. In a way reminiscent of the twenties, people seemed to throw off their cares and set out to enjoy themselves; there was a heady feeling of liberation in the air, for women, students, third world countries and various minority groups.

All these changes had their positive aspects and brought more equality; however there was a price to pay, as in all revolutions, even peaceful ones. "Middle class morality" had long been assailed for humbug and hypocrisy by sceptical and progressive intellectuals, using the potent weapons of social investigation, irony and satire. Now these conventional values were challenged as never before also from below, not only by the traditional ploys of impertinence and lack of deference, but by the active promotion of various sub-cultures, and novel cults of drugs, loud music, pornography and bad language in the arts, literature and entertainment. So much so that many now look back on the swinging sixties and judge them as essentially silly, if not vicious.

The seventies were certainly not much better, for a new sour note crept into controversy and confrontations: a tendency to whinge about everything. In the eighties we have also witnessed a revival of party spirit and spitefulness. These unpleasant features of our time, together with the rise in crime, violence, vandalism, drug-taking and alcoholism, have led many to see signs of decay and decadence. They ask whether we have reached rock bottom yet, so that the only way ahead is out and upwards, or whether there will be a still greater increase in all these evils. It seems that we have at last to wake up and grow up and take full responsibility for our own manners and those of our offspring. We can no longer behave like naughty and immature children ourselves, or depend on socially superior groups to set our standards, blaming everything on the "Nanny state", or the Queen or even Mrs Thatcher – to do so is infantile. We now have duties as well as rights. For we ourselves are always at the frontiers of our own time, the cutting edge of our own society. So nowadays we are all "the makers of manners".

It may seem at first a strange idea that social values, customs and manners may be regarded as creative inventions, quite as much as motor cars or computers, yet somebody had to initiate the party, the barbeque, even the May Ball. Perhaps because women originally developed many aspects of such gracious living, their social achievements have been persistently under-valued, like the skills of tapestry or embroidery, or the variety of "mother tongues" in the world. Therefore, we now have to think out our social values and customs anew and more self-consciously.

So what can be done to improve our politeness and our manners today? Particular campaigns may be of value and particular practical "workshops" for different occupations, as described elsewhere in this book. How can these people – shop assistants, cashiers, factory managers and workers, receptionists, people in the "caring" professions, house-wives, pensioners, help themselves and each other to feel better, happier, kinder to one another? Can such skills really be taught at all? My favourite personal dream is to set up finishing schools for our young men in the inner cities.

My great fear is, however, that all these efforts may prove piecemeal, superficial and transient, because of our failure to address some more basic and underlying problems in our society. For just as it is impossible to have permanent peace between peoples without some basic justice, e.g. in Palestine or South Africa, or to heal a deep wound by simply covering it over with sticking-plaster, so politeness, to be genuine, must arise from a bed-rock of sincere benevolence. For what would be the use of a courtesy campaign in Northern Ireland or the Lebanon? People in those places may in fact be remarkably kind and polite to each other, under such conditions, but the basic problems are not cured thereby, merely the better endured.

What is needed would seem to be rather a master satirist to knock the knockers and mercilessly ridicule sectarian bigotry or, better still, a fearless old hell-fire preacher to denounce the sinful men of violence and call for repentance. Today we shy away from talking about "sins" at all, but in fact, most instances of gross rudeness and callousness are but symptoms of the great classic sins of arrogance, injustice, cruelty and impenitence.

A sound underlying religion or philosophy would seem to be required, but these subjects are currently most grievously neglected in our schools, on the plea that all is relative. So, for instance, today's children are not even well enough informed of their Christian inheritance either to accept or to reject it. Meanwhile, many families have broken down and basic moral teaching also tends to be neglected in our giant comprehensives. Yet children are expected to think out for themselves from scratch an entirely new philosophy of living; a daunting undertaking even for an adult, when even the most original philosophers have, in practice, always built upon classic foundations.

Young people are not assisted in this by many public and political discussions on TV where a lop-sided and sentimental version of humanitarianism is assumed but never defined, so that many issues are blurred. For there is a heavy emphasis on "my" rights and the State's duties *to* me and no counterbalancing emphasis on my "duties" and what society can reasonably expect *of* me. So it is not surprising that much juvenile behaviour appears anarchic, self-indulgent, destructive and amoral, justified, as it is, as legitimate self-expression, or even "a cry for help". It is a cry for help all right, and that help might range from a course in logic to a good hiding.

Now a sound underlying religion or philosophy to guide one through life may take many forms. It could be Christianity of some kind, Judaism, Islam, Hinduism, Buddhism or even Humanism (in the sense of well-considered agnosticism). But whatever it is, it can never be absorbed or practised without effort; that is without study, self-discipline, practical good works and regular prayer or reflection; it cannot simply be left to chance. Thus even the great sceptical philosophers of the 18th century Enlightenment studied the Classics and the Church before they criticised them. Tom Paine read his Bible well before questioning its literal truthfulness, and later higher biblical critics have not only known the scriptures backwards, but been able to read them in the original Hebrew, Greek and Latin, whereas the modern sceptic speaks from ignorance.

Similarly, many aspects of practical religion or good manners are not merely virtues to be "caught" but skills to be definitely taught e.g. the practice of writing letters of thanks for hospitality received or of condolence upon a bereavement. Social events have to be well organised, invitiations written, catering arrangements made, guests welcomed etc. We do not value such skills as we should. But, in the words of the song, "nothing comes from nothing", and in most fields of human endeavour it is still true that the best results come from dedication, discipline and persistence.

After "sins", "duty" is the unmentionable four-letter-word of the late eighties. If you doubt this, try it out on a Sixth Form Class or on your most progressive friends and notice how shocked they are! But Duty, "stern daughter of the voice of God", was not only the very backbone of Victorian morality at its best, but also the key to the whole Humanitarian Movement, and the prime motivation for reformers as diverse as Elizabeth Fry, William Wilberforce, Lord Shaftesbury, Florence Nightingale, General William Booth and David

Livingstone. Duty, I suspect, is also the key to the re-establishment of the gracious, humane and polite society.

1. Penelope Tremayne – Nor Iron Bars a Cage, (Heinemann)
2. The Life of Rufus Isaacs by his son, mentioned in Chesterton's Review

Chapter Seven

MEDIA OBSERVATIONS

Since the formation of the Polite Society in 1986 the media has devoted increasing time and space to discussions of the issues about which we hold firm views.

Prime Minister Mrs Margaret Thatcher is a firm supporter of the ideas which the Polite Society promotes. In the Daily Mail on April 29th 1988, she said:

"The rules of a civilised society are politeness and good neighbourliness. They are fundamental to the environment in which we live.

"Many young people today recognise that you have to have rules by which to live. And they want a kinder discipline, affectionate firmness in the family and at school and at work. They recognise that this is the essence of community living and it is the essence of civilisation."

So she thought good manners were coming back, did she?

"Among some people," she answered. "But there are still many who should know better; who do not respect the community or their neighbours. And it is not just a question of money or of background. It is a question of attitude."

But could she expect everyone to change in a generation?

No, she did not. "I remember my father used to say, "Look, there is a streak of evil in everyone and the essence of life is to teach us that the good things come to the fore and the evil things are restrained." That is what I am talking about. That is what we have got to get through to everyone and establish rules to ensure that this is so."

There were so many institutions in society that could lead us back to a more civilised style of behaviour, she said. This meant living within the generally–accepted rules; most of all thinking about your neighbours and how your actions would impinge on them, and about a generosity of spirit towards other people.

"Civilisation is the responsibility of every single person. George Bernard Shaw said: 'Freedom incurs responsibility. That is why so many men fear it and you cannot have one without the other'.

"The good news is that throughout the whole of our country the majority of people really recognise it. They really do. And the great battle now is to prevent the smaller minority ruining the lives of the majority by violence, by dirtiness, by graffiti, by everyday surliness."

Surliness? "Yes, surliness," she said. "Graciousness has been replaced by surliness in much of everyday life."

Now much of the struggle which we as a nation should commit ourselves to, she went on, was a reversal of that: the replacement of surliness with simple, good-humoured graciousness. There were still plenty of examples through the country, but we needed more. We needed more sporting and show business heroes to set the standards. The older generation of sportsmen and entertainers had developed a natural graciousness and courtesy.

Not so many of the new ones had, but there was no reason why they should not because everyone had a great deal of good and bad in them. And whether you decide to be courteous and pleasant or surly and aggressive was simply a matter of the face you turned to the world. "It's simply the way of life you choose to live."

As Prime Minister she could not single handedly stop crime or indeed even begin to make an impact on the way people treated each other in their everyday lives. She could provide more money for policing and new technology for the forces of law and order, and she did that. But in the end the social order was about individuals sticking to the rules.

It began with unselfishness and decent behaviour towards each other. This had to be taught to the young and emphasised throught their upbringing.

"It requires everyone to be on the side of courtesy,

thoughtfulness, discipline, consideration and care, whether in the churches, the schools, families and institutions. All should say when confronted with bad behaviour: 'Look, you don't do this. You just do not behave like this'."

It sounded perhaps too simple. No, she did not think so. There was a great longing for more pleasant daily behaviour in life. She got that from people she met, and from thousands of letters she received. The problem was to get it across to ordinary people that it was in their own hands.

A culture of courtesy could be reintroduced, and it should begin in the homes and go on through the schools and into university life and then business. It could become ingrained and there were still plenty of societies in the world where it was. And, she repeated, it was natural to the British.

Daily Mail Editor David English commented: "Mrs Thatcher, it seems to me, is searching for a new set of social standards and she wishes to imprint them on the national consciousness before the turn of the century. .. Much would have to be achieved in the nineties, she agreed, but she believed that there was a yearning for a greater decency and thoughtfulness in life and we would see new standards set in the next decade which would take us to the turn of the century, not only as a more prosperous country but a better one. We were now a wealth-creating country and so the climate was right for social and moral regeneration."

From the Sunday Times, July 17 1988:

". . . Economic success, still too short-lived and slender to take for granted, needs to be accompanied by a social and moral revolution. This will be infinitely more difficult to achieve. The social rot has gone deeper than the industrial decay of the 1960s and 1970s, and cannot be cut out with the simpler, crude strokes which proved so effective on the economy . . . But a sharp reversal in the long decline in personal and social standards is imperative all the same. If the long drawn out agony of Britain's economic decline can be reversed, so can the decline of its social morality. The national interest requires it and the coming generation has the right to expect it. But how to do it?

"The first task is to win the argument that it is even possible: most people accept that such an improvement is desperately needed, but many doubt that anything worthwhile can be done. Exhortation alone will achieve nothing: neither will casting blame at other people's doors. We are all responsible . . ."

From the Daily Mail, July 2, 1988:

"Loud and persistent noise is often unbearable and sometimes produces in normally law-abiding people a

96

most violent response. Noise can be every bit as damaging to mental health as a physical attack is to the body, but it is usually more prolonged. To direct such noise at some other human being is an atrocious breach of the good manners on which civilised life depends. It is all a part of the growth of yobbery which increasingly disfigures our society and which we must find ways of quelling if decent, courteous and orderly life in this overcrowded island is to survive."

"Girl About Town", London.

"I have long believed that the single thing which would most improve the world, would be for all of us to be just a little more polite to each other. Without spending a single penny, without hurting anybody, we could have a revolution. Without really changing a thing we could all lead happier, more pleasant, more fulfilling, basically much better, nicer lives. Being polite is simply so easy, yet so remarkably caring for everybody. The difficult thing for me to understand is why everybody does not do it all the time.

"What I mean by being polite has got nothing to do with etiquette or formal good manners. As far as I can see society is far better off for having rejected the rigid, restrictive code which once governed our every move. We have turned our back on the old polite society. But we haven't really replaced it with anything else. Being rude, insensitive, thoughtless, is no way for anybody to live. Unfortunately we do live more and more like that. Genuine, spontaneous politeness, as a matter of course, is simply no longer in fashion.

"I decided, on the day I discovered my new club (The Polite Society) to make an extra special effort to be nice to everybody. It is remarkable what a massive difference it makes. After saying a cheery good morning to people that I normally pass silently on the stairs and receiving rather surprised versions of the same in return, I went out into the big bad world with a smile on my face and a spring in my step. The sun was shining, and I was now shining, too. So I held open a few doors, even though it meant waiting a little to do so. I also adopted the simple tactic of smiling at everybody who caught my eye. And through it all I felt wonderful. And what is more I discovered that politeness is addictive. Everybody I was nice to responded favourably, pleased to be treated with courtesy. One woman who I helped up the stairs on the underground with her shopping said I had made her day. And that honestly made mine. Everywhere I went in London seemed a brighter, friendlier place because I was a brighter friendlier person. At the end of the day without having gone out of my way once, or expended more than the energy it takes to smile, I felt happy and I felt good.

"So why don't we all do it? Excuses about the pace of life being too fast simply will not wear. We all have a second to wish somebody well. Maybe we've stopped doing it because we have forgotten how good it feels. I can assure you how rewarding it is. I don't think we should all become mindless Californians Wishing each other empty good days. We should just have genuine respect for each other . . ."

Robert Elms

Lord Chief Justice Lord Lane told an audience at the opening of a new law courts in Manchester that a "huge wave of crime" was threatening to engulf the country. There had been a general lowering of standards "at every stage of life and at every level".

But by comparison, the 1930s, when unemployment was proportionately as bad as it is now, was a time "of unprecedented lawfulness".

The Lord Chief Justice said that the great 19th century reformers had attributed crime to poverty and filth, appalling housing condition, lack of medical care, indifferent education and the absence of any social services.

"Cure those evils, they thought, and you can close down your prisons," he said.

"The prisons were then no more than a staging post between arrest on the one hand and the gallows and the transportation on the other.

"What would they say now, when we have the welfare state, the Education Act, the Clean Air Act, the National Health Service and three prisoners in cells designed by those very Victorians for the accommodation of one?"

Lord Lane said that in the 1930s, "you had no need to lock your house when you went shopping or to remove the ignition key from your car . . . when you left it."

"Yet unemployment was proportionately as bad as it is now, there was no welfare state, housing conditions were abysmal and the threat of war loomed large over everyone."

Lord Lane said that this was not the time or place to examine the reasons "for the huge wave of crime which threatens to engulf us and has necessitated the provision of many of these new courts."

He added: "There are as many opinions on that subject as there are sociologists. No doubt there has been a general lowering of standards at every stage of life and on every level."

From the Daily Telegraph:

"FIRM, an organisation dedicated to settling disputes without recourse to the law, says a door-to-door survey on one estate in London showed that one resident in four was involved in long-standing disputes with neighbours . . . Many of the disputes began as minor differences. Said Professor Christopher Mitchell, of the City University: 'We have a choice between allowing our communities to fragment in a war of everyone against everyone else, or developing the skills by which people can sort out their differences peacefully and constructively'."

Daily Mail, December 1st 1987.

"From the disgraceful behaviour of England's cricketers in Pakistan, via boardroom chicanery and on-field anarchy in British soccer, and primaeval savagery in rugger, through dubious financial dealings in British athletics and world yachting and perennially murky finances of big boxing, honest people have been asked to swallow the unacceptable . . .

"For decades the sports pages of newspapers were about courage and achievement. They are now about bullies, dissenters, charlatans, thieves, moaners and cheats . . . The way it has been recently, sport as we know it almost invests bullfighting and bear-baiting with some small nobility."

Ian Wooldridge

Chapter Eight

APT COMMENTS . . .

MANNERLY MARRIAGE – *by Irene Thomas – a veteran of 40 years of it, and a Polite Society Life Member.*

It makes one wonder what on earth the children of people who are so constantly hopping from marriage to cohabitation and back again will do when they grow up and become "romantically linked" themselves. Surely some fairly careful investigation will be needed to prevent an ill-advised marriage to a possibly-forgotten half-brother or sister?

But thankfully, to most people, marriage remains a subject for thought and consideration. Anyone who has survived twenty, thirty or forty years of it will tell you that it needs constant care and work. If you are not prepared to commit yourself to all that, then don't marry.

Some modern sages – thankfully fewer each year – will tell you that "marriage is just a piece of paper", and "we are happy as we are". This, to couples who have weathered the storms and sunshine of married life, is a rather juvenile attitude. It is difficult to describe the difference between mere cohabitation and real marriage, except to say that it's like comparing the experience of astronauts in a laboratory simulator, and astronauts actually in orbit!

Of course marriage is not easy. Taking responsibility for somebody else never is. There will be days when you wish you had never undertaken the whole wretched arrangement, but – other than physical violence to either partner – there is nothing that can or should break a marriage that is based on a firm foundation of love, friendship and loyalty.

Ordinary daily life with anyone – husband, wife, parents, brother, sister or flat-mate, is never easy, either. The one infallible "oil" for the wheels of everyday living is true politeness – NOT the icy "hissing-through-clenched-teeth" politeness that some couples display in public, but true consideration for the feelings of one's husband or wife. Don't criticise her clothes in public – you should have given your opinion at home. Don't interrupt his jokes – you may have heard them scores of times, but other people haven't. Dress neatly, keep spotlessly clean (not easy when there are small children in the house!). Compliment each other on any extra effort to look or sound attractive, or on a household task well done. Praise for a good meal, whether cooked by husband or wife or child, is always well received! Remember birthdays and anniversaries – not difficult surely, you've only to write them into each new diary.

But above all LISTEN to each other. Don't necessarily give advice, just listen with a sympathetic ear. Put down your book, switch off the telly, and give him or her your full attention. To have someone "on your side" at home is a recipe for a good marriage, and for good parenthood, too, and can alleviate the stresses of working life.

Children change a couple's life irrevocably, and parents ought to be fully mature themselves before they start a family. All successful parents will know that children are best reared by a mixture of love, discipline and example. Perhaps the last is the most important – and most difficult! – of all. Small boys and girls will copy their parents' attitudes and speech, both towards each other and towards anyone younger, older or weaker than themselves, and they should be taught to ask, "How would I like to be treated in this situation?" That question is the foundation of all good manners.

Home, no matter how simple or spartan, should be a source of warmth and strength. Expensive material possessions are pleasant, but not essential. "Better is a dinner of herbs where love is, than a stalled ox and hatred therewith".

The "ME" generation during the past twenty years or so has produced some graceless and self-centred people – some of them middle-aged now, and as churlish and peevish as they ever were – eternal toddlers, in fact.

But bitter experience has begun to change our outlook, and the next generation can be made aware of how pleasant life can be if each small child could be made to realise that the world does not revolve exclusively around him or her. Surliness must be made unacceptable – not just shrugged off – and then good manners will become as natural as breathing. Our people were once renowned world-wide for their polite and pleasant demeanour, and it would be a happy achievement to regain that reputation.

No true national recovery can take place unless everyone, from grandparent to toddler, does his or her utmost to spread the good word – and the good deed, too!

And it all begins in the home . . .

LOSING MARKS – *by Marjorie Boulton, the author of "The Anatomy of Literary Studies" and marker of thousands of scripts.*

I would never defend the policy of my elementary school, which, even by corporal punishment, imposed one school style of handwriting; I still remember children being shouted at, perhaps with a slap, to finish off every S with a dot at the join! There can be as many styles of writing as there are people; but all the letters should be clearly differentiated and all the words separated.

Illegible handwriting is a form of discourtesy, because it asks the other person to make the effort; which implies that the other person's time is less valuable than that of the scrawler. Several experiments have shown me that to mark a paper or exercise in really bad handwriting takes up to four times as long as to mark one that is, in whatever style, legible.

'A' Level examinations may be vital to someone's career. In my experience, 'A' Level examiners are not allowed to deduct marks for bad handwriting, as a deliberate penalty; but marks do tend to deduct themselves. How? An examiner may be coping with several hundred scripts, all several pages long, and to be marked by a date that approaches alarmingly fast. If that examiner cannot really read an answer as an argument, but has to decipher it word by word and keep losing the thread, the candidate will almost certainly lose by this. If the examiner wonders whether to give, say, 15, 16 or 17 marks to an answer, who is going to get the benefit of the doubt? The candidate whose writing has given no trouble, or the one whose wretched beetle-tracks have cost the examiner already an extra half-hour and irritated tired eyes further? Enormous efforts and careful regulations seek to make the marking of vital examinations as fair as possible; but markers and those who check the marking are all human beings! If there is some doubt about a pass or fail, or a grade and a higher grade, the neat, legible paper will at least keep the awarder in a good mood and ready to look for the decisive extra mark; the paper that takes four times as long to read, perhaps with some words actually unreadable, does not encourage anyone to bother . . .

Illegible handwriting is like mumbled speech: it is a nuisance to other people; but it is also a disadvantage to the perpetrator.

MEN AND WOMEN – *by Mary Kenny, a Patron of the Polite Society who recently wrote in her column in the Sunday Telegraph:*

Are young men nicer to young women today than young men used to be? To hear girls in their twenties talk about men can be an alarming revelation.

Reports of sexual harassment, of appalling bad manners, of brute indifference, constant cadging and a wholesale want of gallantry are what I repeatedly hear. "It appears that 85 per cent of American men expect a woman to go to bed with them on the first date," I remarked to a student in her early twenties, referring to the new and notorious Hite Report on relations between the sexes.

"I wouldn't put it as high as that in England," she replied sardonically. "Here, it is only about 80 per cent."

The Hite Report, recently the cover story of Time magazine, claimed that relationships between the sexes have never before been so poor. Ninety-five per cent of women were said to complain of harassment from men, and 98 per cent said that they wanted to make basic changes in their relationships with men.

The report is undoubtedly exaggerated, but there is evidence that some of it is true. Surveys by Woman's Day, New Woman, Glamour and the Journal of Marriage and the Family came up with findings in a similar vein: that women are deeply dissatisfied with modern men.

What appears to have happened is that the carapace of chivalry, which once somewhat restrained the more brutish aspects of male chauvinism, has been removed, and what emerges is the rampant, uninhibited male, encouraged on all sides to think that females are there for the taking. I have been sceptical, in the past, of claims of sexual harassment; it was, I thought, simply a new word for flirting.

But young women insist that flirting has gone, along with manners, kindness, consideration. Courtship has gone: love-letters have gone: romance has gone. The commercialisation of sex has turned it into just another recreational commodity: "bonking", as it is called in the popular prints, has about as much romantic content as a football game.

"Men today have all the attitudes of the permissive society, and all the same old double standards too," I hear it said. "They expect you to sleep with them straight off, but they still think you're a slag for doing so." The notion that a friendship, a courtship, a relationship should have time to grow and develop is out of style.

It makes my blood boil to see the casualness with

which nice, kindly, sensitive and thoughtful young girls are treated today; not only are they taken for granted, but the beasts leave town without a telephone call or a note of farewell. It seems that in past times we did at least receive the occasional red rose.

SMILES' VIEW

A new edition of Self Help by Samuel Smiles has recently been published by Sidgwick and Jackson in their Library of Management Classics.

It was first published in 1859, and has been reprinted, quoted and translated many times.

Those familiar with the book will know it to be a testimony to the individual, and how far by our own efforts we can rise above the circumstances in which we happen to be born, or to which we appear to be destined.

Smiles may be scorned for his insistence on high moral worth by those who see the real world to have passed on from that simple outlook. But more and more people are now realising that what has replaced it – a cynical determination to "get on" at all costs, or to rely on the welfare benefits made available by others – are deeply unsatisfactory.

In a new introduction, Sir Keith Joseph writes: "Smiles cannot be dismissed as a humbug or as a smug moralist. Of radical inclination, sensitive and compassionate, he believed in the work of ordinary man and in his capacity to realise himself. He judged not in terms of money or social status, but of the fullest use by each individual of every quality, skill and talent he possessed."

Here is a section of the book in which Smiles refers to good manners:

"As daylight can be seen through very small holes, so little things will illustrate a person's character. Indeed, character consists in little acts, well and honourably performed; daily life being the quarry from which we build it up, and rough-hew the habits which form it. One of the most marked tests of character is the manner in which we conduct ourselves towards others. A graceful behaviour towards superiors, inferiors, and equals is a constant source of pleasure. It pleases others because it indicates respect for their personality; but it gives tenfold more pleasure to ourselves. Every man may to a large extent be a self-educator in good behaviour, as in everything else; he can be civil and kind, if he will, though he have not a penny in his purse. Gentleness in society is like the silent influence of light, which gives colour to all nature; it is far more powerful than loudness or force, and far more fruitful. It pushes its way quietly and persistently, like the tiniest daffodil in spring, which raises the clod and thrusts it aside by the simple persistency of growing.

"Morals and manners, which give colour to life, are

of much greater importance than laws, which are but their manifestations. The law touches us here and there, but manners are about us everywhere, pervading society like the air we breathe. Good manners, as we call them, are neither more nor less than good behaviour; consisting of courtesy and kindness; benevolence being the preponderating element in all kinds of mutually beneficial and pleasant intercourse amongst human beings. 'Civility', said Lady Montague, 'costs nothing and buys everything.' The cheapest of all things is kindness, its exercise requiring the least possible trouble and self-sacrifice. 'Win hearts,' said Burleigh to Queen Elizabeth, 'and you have all men's hearts and purses.' If we would only let nature act kindly, free from affectation and artifice, the results on social good humour and happiness would be incalculable.

"The little courtesies which form the small change of life may separately appear of little intrinsic value, but they acquire their importance from repetition, and accumulation.

"The cultivation of manner – though in excess it is foppish and foolish – is highly necessary in a person who has occasion to negotiate with others in matters of business.

"Another mode of displaying true politeness is consideration for the opinions of others. It has been said of dogmatism that it is only puppyism come to its full growth; and certainly the worst form this quality can assume is that of opinionativeness and arrogance. Let men agree to differ, and when they do differ, bear and forbear. Principles and opinions may be maintained with perfect suavity, without coming to blows or uttering hard words; and there are circumstances in which words are blows, and inflict wounds far less easy to heal.

"The inbred politeness which springs from right-heartedness and kindly feelings is of no exclusive rank or station. The mechanic who works at the bench may possess it, as well as the clergyman or the peer. It is by no means a necessary condition of labour that it should, in any respect, be either rough or coarse."

An exchange of correspondence between The Rev. Ian Gregory, Founder of the Polite Society and Avril Cochrane.

Avril Cochrane
Etruria
Stock on Trent
Staffs.

"It is a laudable aim to attempt to promote consideration and respect for others. However, I cannot agree with the point made on the Polite Society's leaflet concerning male members of the society treating women with 'especial courtesy' and 'chivalry'.

"As a woman, I find it most offensive to be treated with excessive politeness (as distinct from normal good manners) solely on the grounds of my sex. It is only too often a means of 'keeping me in my place', and is therefore, in truth, a form of insult.

"Surely, true good manners consists of treating all persons with an equally high degree of courtesy and respect? Thank you for reading this letter."

Rev. Ian Gregory
Basford
Newcastle-u-Lyme
Staffs.

"Thank you for taking the trouble to write to me. The point you make has troubled a small number of the 5,000 people who have written to me about the Polite Society, and I understand it well.

"I take the view that the sensitive nature of relationships between men and women in general calls for a recognition by each of the distinctive role they play in human society. Women, in my view, have a role to play which is different – not more or less important – than that of men. If women will not allow men to treat them with especial consideration then both men and women miss something of great importance in the privilege of being human. I think men miss most: for it is in being allowed to show especial courtesy that they find out what it is to be male in the best possible meaning of the word.

"The resentment which a minority of women now display towards any kind of courteous act leaves a man in some perplexity about who he really is. And in his

114

uncertainty he may turn to the kind of aggressive and silly behaviour which we see in town centres at weekend and on football stadia terraces.

"I entirely agree with you that common courtesies should have no gender barriers, and we should all treat one another with respect and due consideration irrespective of social, sexual or generation difference. But I am quite convinced that the strident feminist has much to answer for in current displays of ill-behaviour. Whatever anybody thinks, Cowper was right in referring to 'the sex that civilises ours'. I fear that we may not have much to agree about, but I am most grateful for your thoughtful comments."

Lou and Antoinette Rezzano and their children

Courtesy Enterprise of the Year

The Cooking Pot Café, Stockport Road, Ardwick Green, Manchester has been named 'Courtesy Enterprise of the Year' after receipt of the following letter, and due inspection:

"As someone who has long despaired of finding courtesy in our society, I felt I must tell you, reverend, of the immense amount of kindness and concern that I have found. I live in Ardwick Green, Manchester, and often visit the Cooking Pot Café on the Stockport Road. It is a very busy family concern. But each customer receives great care. Not only is the food delicious but the owner and his wife and daughters are the most wonderfully kind, considerate and polite people I have ever met. Money is not demanded: they have a 'special' way of making it a pleasure to pay (a cheap price for an excellent service). I have been treated to teas and coffees many a time. Such wonderful people should gain some recognition. To sit in their shop and see how they behave, not only to their customers, but the immense love for each other, is a joy. Even the most awkward of customers is worked upon until he realises that he need not be nasty. For two young girls the owner's daughters are wonderful. They show great respect for their parents and customers, and have respect for each other. When they bought the café, it had no trade; now I think sometimes that they feed the whole of Manchester, it seems so busy. The owners are always in the same good mood; happy to be there, valuing their customers as friends. Efficiency is certainly achieved but by no means surrendering their courtesy. They all look genuinely happy to see every customer. These are obviously people touched by God's message."

E.M. Barnes

A Polite Society Inspector, Jackie Whittaker, commented:

"The Cooking Pot Café is run by husband and wife team Lou and Antoinette Rezzano with help from relatives and friends. During the past twelve months since taking over the café the couple have built up a reputation for providing good food at reasonable prices, which is always served with a smile and a courteous word. Before the Rezzano's took over, the café was run down and easily passed by. Now drivers from London, Leicester and Birmingham make detours of many miles to eat at The Cooking Pot, where their cups of tea are legendary and their bacon butties sizzling, but it is the warm welcome and good service which wins the loyalty of all customers.

'We always try to have a nice word with everyone,' said Mrs Rezzano. 'Some people have travelled many

118

miles, and are in need of a rest, good food and a little friendship'."

Mr Rezzano wrote in response:

"We were delighted to hear about the award and very surprised too. It's the best thing to have happened to us for a long time, and it makes all our efforts to provide a good service seem worthwhile. We will always keep Mr Barnes' letter and we will never forget the lovely things he wrote about us. In our hearts we will share the award with our customers, they deserve it much more than we do. They have been marvellous to us. Every morning at 6 a.m. they are already waiting for us on the doorstep, and we look forward to starting the day.

"Looking back to when we had our first café near Wigan before the children were born, we were very lucky there too with the customers. Many of them became friends and occasionally we will see a familiar face from the old days in Wigan coming in the café. It has been over twenty years but we always recognise each other, and we are still as fortunate with customers, they are a pleasure to serve. Working days go very quickly for us, our children Julie (20), Jill (18) and Mark (13), although they are all still studying, help us whenever they can.

"God bless,

Antonietta and Louis Rezzano, Julie, Jill and Mark"

Eric Green, who runs a cycle firm in Ambergate, Derbyshire writes:

"The postman came. I ran downstairs. At last, the small parts I'd ordered for my friend's scooter had arrived.

"But the firm had sent the wrong part; an inner instead of an 'outer' was enclosed.

"My feelings rose. I'd write and give them a blast-off. After all, I'd so clearly explained it over the phone. But politeness came to the fore.

"Dear Sirs, (I wrote) Thank you for your prompt attention. But I'm afraid you've sent an 'inner' instead of an 'outer'. However, I'll keep the part for my stock. Please send me the correct item. I enclose the broken part to help you select the right spare. Thank you again . . . etc.

"So, God came to my rescue in the very nick of His Good Time. He couldn't have picked a better moment to rub in the fact that 'Politeness Always Pays'.

"Could Jesus ever have said to the Leper, 'Hop it, you filthy old geezer?' Jesus was the most polite, even in front of Pilate.

"And Jesus suffered more than just obtaining the wrong spare part!"

Schools

THE FOLLOWING SCHOOLS are in corporate membership of the Polite Society. Teachers write to say that membership is a positive incentive for children to observe simple rules of polite behaviour in their daily life.

Grindleton CE Primary School, near Clitheroe, Lancs
(Head teacher Mr S Lievesley)

Westfield County Infants School, Hinckley, Leicestershire
(Head teacher Mrs M S Janaway)

Ightham Primary School, Sevenoaks, Kent
(Contact Mrs D W Comonte)

Windlaw Primary School, Castlemilk, Glasgow
(Class teacher Mrs H Broadley)

Torquay Boys' Grammar School
(Contact Dylan James)

Ancrum Primary School, Jedbergh
(Head teacher Mrs Judith Caulfield)

Reaside Middle School, Rednal, Birmingham
(Teacher Susie Stockton-Link)

Primrose Hill Junior School, Regents Park, London
(Class teacher Rita McGuire)

Sandown Primary School, Hastings, E.Sussex
(Deputy Head teacher D Henty)

Tittensor First School, Tittensor, Stoke on Trent
(Contact parent S Hibbert)

Oreston County Primary School, Plymouth
(Teacher Mrs Mary Hough)

Hutton Cranswick County Primary School, Driffield, N Humberside (Head teacher D Shimmin)

Barclay Junior School, Leyton, London
(Head teacher J C Cullis)

In addition the 1st Ashtead Guide Co, (Miss N M Ashbee) of Ashtead, Surrey, have also joined, as have members of

M and B Leisure, Glasgow Cross

ADDRESSES

PART TWO

COURTESY ENTERPRISES are either nominated for inclusion in the Guide, or apply for recognition and undergo incognito inspection. The exclusion of any business or service does not imply criticism of its standards. Nominations for future editions are welcomed.

SOUTH EAST

Enterprises at Alresford Hampshire were inspected by the Polite Society at the invitation of the local Chamber of Trade. Very high marks were given after scrupulous consideration on the criteria of courtesy and cheerful service. In some cases constructive criticism was offered to certain shops in confidence.

Anderson's Fish Shop,
West Street,
Alresford

> Attractively dressed windows. Helpful re fish preparation and cooking.

D Gedye Electrical,
Broad Street,
Alresford,

> Very obliging. Demonstrated equipment most willingly.

Stiles China Shop,
Broad Street,
Alresford,

> Allowed to browse. Immaculate appearance. Clean carpet.

Portman Building Society,
5 West Street,
Alresford.

> Excellent overall impression.

A and S Fruiterers,
West Street,
Alresford.

> Wares well displayed. Swept up pile of veg "tops" next to front door detracted from appearance. Most staff charming.

Jeffrey P. Webb Esq.,
Harvest Delicatessen,
West Street,
Alresford.

> Food so tempting that customers waited their turn patiently. Only one staff and five waiting but assistant remained pleasant and gave personal service.

Candover Gallery,
West Street,
Alresford,

> Staff and premises outstanding in every respect.

Watercress Travel,
West Street,
Alresford.

> Very interested to give
> information and service
> even though we explained
> we were just "passing
> through" and would not
> be booking a holiday.

Newsmann,
6 West Street,
Alresford.

> Propietor Mr Mann is
> proud of relationship with
> customers. Inspector
> impressed by layout and
> clear notices.

Home Bakery,
West Street,
Alresford.

> Owner and shop neat,
> tidy and attractive. Very
> good selection of birthday
> cakes.

Home Styles,
Broad Street,
Alresford,

> Very willing to help when
> customers inquire.

Kitchen Elegance,
34 West Street,
Alresford,

> Questions answered in
> detail.

Tapestry Centre,
West Street,
Alresford.

> Very obliging, even when
> we made it clear we were
> not buying

Pastimes,
West Street,
Alresford.

> Very chatty. Superb
> collection of teddy bears.
> Leisurely atmosphere.

Little Sisters Restaurant,
West Street,
Alresford.

> Served coffee willingly.
> Toilets exceptionally
> clean. Music somewhat
> intrusive.

Buckley, Chemist,
224 Barnett Wood Lane,
Ashtead, Surrey.

> ... unfailing courtesy and
> consideration for all, and
> capably applied
> knowledge ...

Winifred Medland

The Granary,
Butcher's Road,
Banbury,
Oxon.

> Everybody is welcomed
> with courtesy and
> patience including
> handicapped people and
> my own guide dog
> puppies.
>
> *Elizabeth Williams*

Safeways Superstore,
22 Greyfriars,
Bedford.

> It is a pleasure to shop in
> this caring store. Very
> cheerful and helpful
> staff.
>
> *Mrs C Sloman*

Tal Thaper Bros.,
Grocery Store,
Grosvenor Road off licence,
Grosvenor Road,
Aldershot,
Hants.

> Always a smiling face . . .
>
> *Albert Fremlin –*
> *Bailey*

Doctor's Surgery,
39 Sea Road,
Bexhill on Sea,
East Sussex.

> A well deserved local
> reputation for being civil
> to everybody under all
> circumstances.
>
> *Polite Society inspector*

Bradford and Bingley Building Society,
581 Christchurch Road,
Boscombe,
Bournemouth.

> Never too busy to count
> £20 loose change, with a
> smile and a joke on a
> busy Saturday morning.
>
> *Evelyn W Rawlings*

Charlie Cars,
Yeomans Industrial Estate,
Bournemouth.

> The boys and girls who
> run these little buses are
> first class. Very kind
> drivers always make sure
> everybody is comfortably
> seated before whizzing
> away. So cheerful and
> obviously happy in their
> jobs – it radiates.
>
> *Marjorie Spiridakis*

Crescent Butchers,
Christchurch Road,
Boscombe,
Bournemouth.

Michael House has a cheerful disposition, extended to every customer. Every regular is known by name and he remembers what you last purchased. A top man who deserves red carpet treatment . . .

Regular customers via
"Streetlife"
Bournemouth

S.M. Pinegar, Butcher,
Ewell Road,
Cheam Village,
Surrey.

Outstanding example of good manners and service.

John Hill

The Fruit Bowl,
Greengrocer,
Station Way,
Cheam Village,
Surrey.

Mr Offer is an outstanding example of good manners and service.

John Hill

Country Fare,
Main Road,
Huntington,
Chichester,
W.Sussex

Unfailingly helpful and cheerful courtesy by all the staff.

Rosemary Muller

5 + 2 Christian Coffee Shop,
Ducking Stool Lane,
Christchurch,
Hants.

Great help to young mothers with babies . . . such kindness.

Kath Watt

Cornerstone Abbey National
                    Estate Agents,
235 Fairmile Road,
Christchurch,
Hants.

Martyn Hogg and secretary Karen were at all times polite, pleasant, patient and caring. I wholeheartedly nominate them.

Mrs J. M. Brooks

Samuel and Mary Collins,
NSS Newsagents,
Fairmile Parade,
Christchurch,
Hampshire.

> Even when busy they
> remain pleasant and
> unflustered and have
> time for a kind word or
> two with every customer.
>
> *Mrs Rosemarie Emmett*

Jenny Knowles,
Olivers Orchard Farm Shop,
Olivers Orchards,
Olivers Lane,
Stanway,
Colchester,
Essex.

> So very helpful and polite
> and always happy.
>
> *W . A. Sibley*

Sandra Valente,
Scruples,
31 Stoke Road,
Gosport,
Hants.

> The staff are always
> friendly and courteous
> and they provide free
> cups of coffee and
> magazines with sherry at
> Christmas.
>
> *Patricia M . Wharton*

Abbey National Building
Society
18 Duke Street,
Henley on Thames.

> Consistently welcoming,
> friendly and polite.
>
> *Lt. Col. P. Harris*

Patisserie Franco-Belge,
45 Bell Street,
Henley on Thames,
Oxon.

> Baking excellent breads
> and taking an interest in
> individual customers;
> always polite. They get on
> quickly but never at the
> expense of the customer
> being served.
>
> *Lt. Col. P. Harris*

Eight of Harts,
8 Hart Street,
Henley on Thames
Oxon

> Cards and confectionery.
> Relaxed, pleasant,
> courteous in a bright
> welcoming atmosphere.
>
> *Lt. Col. P. Harris*

Waitrose Superstore,
Henley on Thames.

> Staff training leads to a
> very high standard of
> courtesy.
>
> *Lt. Col. P . Harris*

The Three Swans Pub/Hotel,
High Street,
Hungerford,
Berkshire.

> The atmosphere is
> friendly, and the staff are
> cheerful, helpful and
> polite.
>
> *A customer*

K. and G. Edwards,
Newsagent,
Sunmead Parade,
Guildford Road,
Leatherhead,
Surrey.

> Always a pleasure to shop
> here ... the customer
> comes first.
>
> *M . Dorothy Brand*

Beachcomber Hotel,
3 Royal Esplanade,
Westbrook,
Westgate on Sea.

> Such a smile. Every
> consideration.
>
> *Helen and Stan Brett*

Gilbert's Bakers,
1155 London Road,
Leigh on Sea,
Essex.

> Always a happy face and
> urgency to serve.
>
> *W. A. Sibley*

Leigh Delicatessen,
107 Broadway,
Leigh on Sea,
Essex.

> Two young ladies who are
> so happy and pleasant all
> the time. Take as much
> trouble about selling 2oz
> coffee as about a whole
> side of smoked salmon.
>
> *W. A. Sibley*

William Sibley,
Nurseryman,
31 Grasmead Avenue,
Leigh on Sea,
Essex.

> Exemplary – a sincere
> interest in all customers
> and their requirements.
>
> *Polite Society inspector*

Michael J,
Hairdresser,
George's Hill,
Widmer End,
Bucks.

> *Recommended by*
> *Angela Lockwood*

Simpson and Barnes,
Gents Outfitters,
Broadway West,
Leigh on Sea.

> Exceptional service. I
> have been most
> impressed.
>
> *June F. Back*

Freezer Shop,
North End,
Portsmouth.

> All youngsters; a pleasure
> to go in there and get a
> friendly smile.

> *Mrs Newman*

Leo's Delicatessen
96 Parkway,
Camden Town,
London.

> Very polite, and helpful
> with customers' bags.

> *H.L*

Print Station,
46 Parkway,
Camden Town,
London.

> An oasis of helpfulness
> and cheerfulness in a
> rather bad mannered
> area.

> *H. L*

Mandeer Restaurant,
21 Hanway Place,
London.

> Superb vegetarian food,
> friendly service and
> advice.

> *Alan Grubb*

Paxton and Whitfield Ltd.,
Cheesemongers,
96 Jermyn Street,
London.

> The patience and
> courtesy shown by every
> member of staff here just
> cannot be bettered.

> *P. M. Ainge*

RCI Europe Ltd.,
Parnell House,
19-28 Wilton Road,
London.

> Holiday exchange;
> Friendly manner of
> everyone from
> receptionist to exchange
> co-ordinator makes for a
> great holiday. It would be
> pleasing to see these
> people recognised for
> their hard work for
> hundreds of happy
> timeshare owners.

> *Mrs. Kay Fussey*

Brian Legon, Esq.,
Mann Egerton and Co. Ltd.,
1085/1095 High Road,
Whetstone,
London.

> Excellent service;
> impressed by their
> attention.

> *E. G. Pearce*

F. G. Curtis & Co. Ltd.,
212 Durnsford Road,
Wimbledon,
London.

Very courteous, and with good relationships within the company. Absolutely outstanding in every way.

Polite Society member

Mrs. H. Staples. 'Choice' Dry Cleaning,
Hayerstock Hill,
London.

Unfailing good manners and warmth from all staff. When they ask how one is they actually want to know.

Mrs. D. Davies-Rees

Camden Hopper Buses,
London Transport.

Drivers have been found to be consistently friendly and courteous.

Miss Alison Malcolm

Barclay's Bank,
69 Plumstead Common Road,
London.

Without the help of Mr Howard and Mr McAvoy during the last six months life would have been very difficult. Outstanding in every way.

Irene Crompton

Ansell and Sons,
Butchers,
5 High Street,
Maldon,
Essex.

No customer's name is ever forgotten; all are of equal importance and their personal attention and service is much appreciated.

D. and G. McLellan

Messrs Tudor Williams Ltd.,
Department Store,
High Street,
New Malden,
Surrey.

They still display the "old fashioned" courtesy and interest which was the norm when the business was established long ago.

Mrs M.W. Picco

Hair Design,
2, Norris Road,
Parkstone,
Poole,
Dorset.

Mr Peter Ryan made me feel at home, as though I had known him all my life. I was treated like somebody important although I am only a pensioner.

Mrs P. Cafe

Lloyd's Bank,
Penn Hill,
Parkstone,
Poole,
Dorset.

Warm, welcoming atmosphere from staff who always seem to be extremely happy – Rosie Jenkins, Christiane Readhead and David Shenton. It rubs off onto customers and I always feel better for having been in – even if to draw money OUT!

Mrs C. Hopkinson

Parkstone Decor,
Ashley Road,
Parkstone,
Poole,
Dorset.

Les always has time for you with help and advice, and makes my day with his humour and friendliness.

Mrs T. Price

G. and D. Butchers,
15 West Street,
Portchester,
Hants.

Customers and courtesy go hand in hand in this shop.

Mrs. D. Williams

Cantoy,
London Road,
North End,
Portsmouth.

Joyce and Teresa sell papers, mags, chocs, sportswear and greetings cards at this large store. They greet everybody with a super smile ... It is always YOU who matters.

Mrs Patricia Ward

Colin Preshop,
Heritage Pine,
954 Brighton Road,
Purley,
Surrey.

I asked if he would give or sell me a spray of blue dyed flowers from the window. He climbed in and got the flowers and refused any payment.

Miss Helen Hoar

Railway Station,
Whytecliffe Road,
Purley,
Surrey.

Most helpful and take a lot of trouble.

Anon

134

Simpson and Barnes,
Gents Outfitters,
109 Broadway West,
Leigh on Sea.

Exceptionally good
service.

June F. Back

Sainsbury's Store,
High Street,
Purley,
Surrey.

Staff very helpful and go
out of their way to show
you where things are.

H. Hoar

Whitley Wood Garage,
Basingstoke Road,
Reading.

Always helpful and
courteous and go out of
their way to help.

Diane E. Whaley

British Home Stores,
Broad Street,
Reading.

When we found a light
fitting part missing I telephoned the manager. He
was very pleasant, sent
the part by taxi and
telephoned later to
ensure that all was well.

Mrs. Joy Jones

Heelas Dept. Store,
Broad Street,
Reading.

*Recommended by a
member*

Ernest Doe and Sons Ltd.,
Weir Pond Road,
Rochford,
Essex.

Agricultural merchants.
So helpful; never too busy
for a laugh and a joke.

W. A. Sibley

Waitrose Supermarket,
1 Ermine Close,
Mayne Avenue,
St. Albans.

Staff unfailingly visible,
cheerful, friendly, helpful
and knowledgeable ...
I've not yet seen or heard
a disgruntled assistant –
even under provocation!

Amber Close

Waitrose Supermarket,
Verulam Street,
St. Albans.

The one and only shop I
know where all customers
are treated alike and with
the greatest respect.

Mrs. M. Fisher

Village Stores,
R. A. Hudson,
Ashmore,
Salisbury,
Wilts.

Always cheerful and
painstaking.

A. M. McCraith

Spar Grocers,
East Beach Road,
Selsey,
West Sussex.

Nothing is any trouble.
They bring things round
with a smile at any time.

Mrs. H. Currie

Education Department,
Standford Prison,
Sheerness,
Kent.

Courtesy and respect
under potentially tricky
conditions for teaching.

John Miles

D.H. Dalzell, Esq.,
Mercury Cycles,
24-26 Heralds Way,
South Woodham Ferrers,
Essex.

John and Doma Dalzell
are polite and extremely
helpful.

William Hadley

Grand Hotel,
Swanage,
Dorset.

A most polite welcome
for four senior citizens,
which made our day when
we called in for a bar
snack.

Mrs A. M. Tuck

Vidcam UK
1A Langton Road,
Tunbridge Wells

Mr Myers delivered to us
on Christmas eve a video
and TV for the children as
ours broke down at 9.00
p.m. Wonderful!

Mrs R. A. Wall

The Best China Shop,
St Alban's Street,
Weymouth,
Dorset.

... very helpful and
courteous: proprietors Mr
and Mrs Masters do not
press you to buy.

Mrs M. Gibson

They have the rare knack
within a few moments of
making you feel that you
are very old friends ...

Mr W. Wade

Neal's Garage,
Abbotsbury Road,
Weymouth,
Dorset.

> . . . I have been a customer for close on 30 years and have always received unfailing courtesy and consideration from proprietor Andrew Neal, his wife Jane, and their assistants.
>
> *W. J. Newman*

Sainsbury's Store,
Badgers Farm,
Winchester.

> Staff always cheerful, no matter what. You name it, they are IT!
>
> *Mrs. M. Holt*

Avant Garde,
Hairdressers,
191 Seabourne Road,
Southborne,
Bournemouth.

> . . . after saying 'thank you' for good hairdressing you get 'You're welcome' . . . what a nice change.
>
> *Mrs Linda Savage*

Gammon and Smith,
Timber and Builders'
Merchants,
Bedford Road,
Petersfield,
Hampshire.

> Bowled over by the good manners and integrity I found here. Even the delivery man said they were a good firm to work for. A pleasure to do business with Mr Keith Wright, Mr Crabtree and their telephone girls.
>
> *Miss Grace E. Moore*

HMS Victory Restaurant,
Naval Dockyard,
Portsmouth.

> Every member of staff has a smile for the jaded customer, which sometimes must be difficult. Most struck by the pleasant demeanour of these young girls and how hard they all work. Worth the rather high prices to be treated as a human being rather than the faceless source of folding money.
>
> *Bernard T. Collard*

SOUTH WEST

Tony's of Larkhall,
Greengrocer, Wholefood,
Pet Food,
Larkhall,
Bath.

Our favourite; cheerful,
friendly and polite

B. C. Hungerford

Automobile Association Centre,
Canal Walk,
Brunel Centre,
Swindon.

Exceptionally busy, but
staff always polite and
efficient.

Anon

W. J. Dickenson Esq.,
Bear Hotel,
Market Square,
Devizes,
Wilts.

Staff are polite cheerful
and efficient. They make
guests feel welcome.

Anon

C and P Motors,
Sandpit,
Clyst St. Mary,
Near Exeter,

Friendly advice, obvious
desire to help and
reliability.

Mrs B. D. White

Walker and Ling,
Fashions,
High Street,
Weston super Mare,
Avon.

Friendly courteous and
helpful. No black looks if
you don't make a
purchase.

Mrs Rachel Heath

Tesco,
Weston Super Mare,
Avon.

Always a cheery greeting
at the checkout and if you
ask where a product is
they take you right to it

Mrs Rachel Heath

Walkers the Bakers.
Kendrick Street,
Stroud,
Gloucestershire.

Staff outstanding in their
willingness to be helpful
at all times.

Dorothy M. G. Binns

Spilsbury's of Clevedon,
93 Hill Road,
Clevedon,
Avon.

I have never ever seen so
many happy faces, of
people actually wanting
to be of service.

Mrs. Molly Cook

Alexander Demaret Esq.,
Alexander Hair and Beauty,
30A Park Street,
Bristol.

Well judged and
carefully applied skills in
human relationships
make a visit here a
unique experience of
warm welcome.

Polite Society Inspector

V and K Langbridge,
4 & 5 Langbridge Bldgs,
St. Saviour's Road,
Larkhall,
Bath,
Avon.

Unfailingly helpful,
friendly and respectful
service in an efficiently-
run well stocked store.

Mrs. B. C. Hungerford

Berkeley Shop,
7 Rolle Street,
Exmouth,
Devon.

Staff give good clean
service as bakers.

Mr. and Mrs. Ian Talbot

Ashley Olsen fruit and veg.,
70 Silver Street,
Nailsea,
Bristol.

Most obliging ... know
customers by name.

Eric S. Smith

Cotswold House Hotel and
Restaurant,
Chipping Camden,
Glos.

Good reputation for
thoughtful and well
managed hospitality.

J. Archibald

No. 19,
Records, tapes etc.,
The Pollet,
St. Peter Port,
Guernsey.

Though aimed at young
people selling records,
tapes, etc., they are always
extremely willing to serve
older people with
courtesy and
consideration

E. A. Bainbridge

Cross Keys Public House,
Taunton,
Somerset.

Efficient barbecue and
splendid attitudes.

G. Browne

Carpenter's Arms,
Lower Metherell,
Callington,
Cornwall.

Prompt courteous service
with a smile from landlord
Douglas Brace.

T. Geddie

Clevelands Country House Hotel,
Steep Hill,
Maidencombe,
Torquay.

We highly recommend
Mr. and Mrs. A. J. Grops –
a grand couple.

*Mr.and
Mrs.L.H.Perkins*

Tesco Store,
Whiddon Valley,
Barnstaple,
Devon.

Always helpful and above
all smiling and friendly
even when working under
great pressure

Mrs.A.G.Watts

Post Office,
New Street,
Painswick,
Stroud,
Glos.

Even when particularly
busy, Mrs. Grey and staff
are always courteous and
helpful

Dorothy B.G.Binns

David Felce, Mobile Fish Merchant,
Water Lane Farm,
Humphries End,
Randwick,
Stroud,
Glos.

Mr. Felce and daughters
and son travel the villages
and are invariably
courteous, friendly and
helpful.

Tesco's
Lee mill,
Ivybridge,
South Devon.

Very keen on courtesy to
customers. People are
sent in pretending to be
customers just to make
sure they are keeping up
the standards.

Mrs M.I.Tubman

Chung Ying Chinese Restaurant,
Factory Row,
Torquay.

Neat and clean and the
waiters extremely
pleasant and eager to
please.

Miss Joy Bicknell

142

The Post Office,
Ashton Gate,
192, Coronation Road,
Bristol.

> Brenda and John Rose
> are never too busy to be
> kind and supportive,
> especially to the elderly.

Meg Webb

Remuera Hotel,
Northfield Road,
Minehead,
Somerset.

> A very friendly and
> courteous hotel.

Anon

THE MIDLANDS

E. J. Couchman, Men's Wear,
422 Birmingham Road,
Wylde Green,
Nr. Sutton Coldfield.

> I stand up for my unsung hero husband. Never without a smile, a happy outlook on life. People often ask me if he is always happy and smiling. I tell them yes ... I have been married to him for 46 years
>
> *Joyce W. Couchman*

Dr. Thomson,
Stafford Road,
Cannock,
Staffs,

> Receptionists are good manners themselves. They put you at your ease and are perfect in every way. The doctor always has time to listen to you.
>
> *Mrs. F Holston*

Mrs. E. Slater,
Hairdresser,
Meadow Road,
Beeston Rylands,
Notts.

> Deserves great admiration for wonderful courtesy. Spotlessly clean, friendly salon.
>
> *Miss C. L. Maher*

Doctor's Surgery,
Shaw Lane,
Albrighton,
Nr. Wolverhampton.

> We are all very grateful for and proud of this great team of doctors, nurses and receptionists.
>
> *John E. Evans*

Staffordshire Building Society,
High Street,
Albrighton,
Wolverhampton.

> Manager and his staff are always courteous and have a cheerful manner to all.
>
> *J. Evans*

Truly Scrumptious,
South Street,
Ilkeston,
Derbyshire.

> A delight to go in. You always feel you are a special customer in this delicatessen.
>
> *Miss M. Walker*

Co-op Bank,
Vision Hire Shop,
Trident Centre,
Dudley,
W. Midlands.

> Good quality service. Always extremely pleasant.
>
> *Mrs. M. Glover*

Brindleys Fashions,
Babington Lane,
Derby.

> Run by the family.
> Reputation impeccable
> and ready and willing to
> serve
>
> *Mr.and Mrs.D.A. and
> K.W.L.Pepper*

Chatsworth House Trust
Chatsworth House
Chatsworth
Bakewell,
Derbyshire.

> Magnificance is matched
> by kindness and civility of
> staff.

Corner Shop,
(Vic and Margaret Brailsford)
79 Lynncroft,
Eastwood,
Notts.

> Never too busy for a
> friendly greeting.
>
> *Mrs. Peggy Webb*

Nat West Bank,
High Street,
Newcastle under Lyme,
Staffs.

> Apparently content to be
> the Polite Society's
> bankers – and cheerfully
> willing to re-calculate
> deposit statements. I
> salute them all.
>
> *Ian Gregory*

Wilcox Desk Top,
Unit 1,
Greenhill Industrial Estate,
Kidderminster,
Worcs.

> I recently did business
> with Wilcox and found
> them most helpful – an
> example to all!
>
> *Susie Stockton-Link*

Sketchley Cleaners,
High Street,
Rowley Regis,
Warley,
W. Midlands.

> Very patient. Will listen
> to anything you say.
> Never keep you waiting.
> Any problem is dealt with
> with minimum fuss.
>
> *Mrs. M. Glover*

Jack Godfrey Removals,
6 Main Street,
Findern,
Derbys.

> We have always found
> this family run firm very
> helpful. Never late!
>
> *B. Smith*

147

Crusty Batch,
Stratford Road,
Shirley,
Solihull.

> Service, hospitality and
> pleasant conversation.

D.B.Drake

Yves Saint Laurent Counter,
Rackham's Store,
Birmingham.

> Absolutely fantastic;
> always laughing , and very
> caring people.

B.Macpherson

Roy Pollard Ltd.,
1756 Coventry Road,
Sheldon,
Birmingham.

> I took a 20 year old
> portable radio to several
> 'chains' for repair but
> they were not interested.
> Roy Pollard could hardly
> believe the radio was still
> around after 20 years.
> Happily fixed it twice in
> six months for no charge.
> It was a gift from my
> father and had
> sentimental value. They
> took time and trouble to
> do a small job at no cost
> to keep one customer
> happy

Miss M. E. R. Thompson

The Polite Society declared Shrewsbury the winner of a National award in 1987. The local council graciously accepted an inscribed trophy, and the Shrewsbury Chronicle most generously sponsored inspection of local businesses which expressed interest. We were pleased to present certificates to the following concerns in or near this superlative old town;

G.A.Hill Esq.,
J.H.Jones Furnishings,
51/52 Mardol,
Shrewsbury.

Radbrook Hall Hotel,
Radbrook Road,
Shrewsbury.

Stephen and Ann Bromley,
Butterfly World,
Yockleton,
Shrewsbury.

Chris Thomas Esq.,
Manager,
Royal Bank of Scotland plc.,
6 The Square,
Shrewsbury.

Copy-Write,
6 High Street,
Shrewsbury.

R.D.Hall Esq.,
Sales Director,
Tanners Wines Ltd.,
26 Wyle Cop,
Shrewsbury.

Proprietor,
Cotswolds Sheepskins and
Woollens,
13 The Square,
Shrewsbury.

F.E. and A. C. Weston,
Goodlife Wholefood
Restaurant,
Barracks Passage,
730 Wyle Cop,
Shrewsbury.

Mrs. L. Davison,
Shropshire Oven,
19 Mardol,
Shrewsbury.

Mrs. M.T. Musker,
Abbotts Mead Hotel,
St. Julian Friars,
Shrewsbury.

M.T.Salomonson Esq.,
Lion Hotel,
Wyle Cop,
Shrewsbury.

Lloyd and Ann Nutting,
Bicton Heath Post Office,
Welshpool Road,
Bicton Heath,
Shrewsbury.

Shrewsbury Tourism,
Guildhall,
Dogpole,
Shrewsbury.

Coleman Brothers (Tamworth) Ltd.,
Market Street,
Tamworth,
Staffs.

Wonderful old fashioned obliging hardware shop.

Mr.and Mrs.D.A. and K.W.L.Pepper

E.M.Jerrams and Co.Ltd.,
Hardware,
High Street,
Measham,
Leicestershire.

No take it or leave it attitude here; they want your custom

Mr.and Mrs.D.A. and K.W.L.Pepper

Peter N. Corlyon, of Cotteridge, Birmingham, took great trouble to make a series of recommendations. Here is a selection of them, which he rated as 'excellent' for always smiling and offering friendly service:

G. Whitcombe,
Baker's Butchers,
199 Church Road,
Yardley

David John,
Butchers,
Stratford Road,
Shirley,
Solihull.

Lawson and Oldridge,
Butchers,
437 Bordesley Green,
Birmingham.

E. Dorman (Mrs. L. Darby, Proprietor),
25 Church Road,
Yardley.

I moved from there two years ago but have been back more than 100 times for smiling service.

Erdington Aquatic Centre,
Church Road,
Erdington,
Birmingham.

   Magnificent.

C.P.Vickerstaff,
Fishmongers Stall 214,
Bull Ring Market,
Birmingham.

Stechford Post Office (Mrs. M.
Boland, Manageress for past 12
years),
153 Albert Road,
Stechford,
Birmingham.

Village Bakery,
Albert Road,
Stechford.

Melvyn's hairdresser,
Richmond Road,
Stechford.

   Professional and friendly.

Vono Bedding Centre,
Stratford Road,
Shirley.
(Under its present courteous
manager).

Malcolm Campbell,
Wool Shop,
11 Watford Road,
Cotteridge,
Birmingham.

Candy Cards,
12 Watford Road,
Cotteridge,
Birmingham.

Mills Photography,
86 The Green,
Kings Norton,
Birmingham.

Goodies,
Office stationery supplies,
23 Watford Road,
Cotteridge,
Birmingham.

Cotteridge Hot Bread Shop,
9 Watford Road,
Cotteridge,
Birmingham

The Country Cupboard,
Health Foods Store,
94 The Green,
Kings Norton,
Birmingham.

Sikkens Paints (UK) Ltd.,
670 Kingsbury Road,
Tyburn,
Birmingham

   Smiling service and
   professional advice.

Mick and Stella's Fried Fish
Shop,
Garrett's Green Lane,
Sheldon,
Birmingham.

151

Raj Poot Indian Restaurant,
Pershore Road,
Cotteridge.

Excellent atmosphere

Wilshere Baldwin and Co.,
Stockbrokers,
19 The Crescent,
King Street,
Leicester.

Very pleasant and well
mannered and always
greet you with a smile ...

Anon

Lake Hotel,
Rudyard,
Nr. Stoke on Trent.

Mr. and Mrs. Ron Lloyd
have changed the image
of the place and it is now
an asset to the whole
village.

Mary Hudson

Springfield Pharmacy,
818 Stratford Road,
Sparkhill,
Birmingham.

A warm welcome,
farewell, cheerfulness and
a seat. What else can one
ask?

Mrs. A.A. Shah

Doctors' Surgery,
6 Bellevue,
Edgbaston,
Birmingham. B5

For the past six years I
have suffered from an
illness which makes it
necessary for me to visit
the doctor sometimes
once or twice a week. I
have no relatives who
could have supported me
through all this, but my
doctor and all his staff
have treated me like the
family I don't have. The
doctor always greets me
with a smile and opens
and closes the door for
me. He is dedicated to his
work and his staff follow
the example. Last week I
made a cake and took it
to the surgery and we all
shared it together. The
surgery is right in the
middle of Birmingham
city centre and life is very
fast in the city. But this
surgery still has time and
most of all the staff see
each patient as an
individual. Sometimes my
illness has made me feel
like giving up, and if the
doctor had not given me
support with kindness
and understanding I
think I might have. The
receptionists are Norma,
Pat, Vanessa, Mandy and
Janet.

Elaine Dalziel

Peter Lister Esq.,
Roebuck Hotel,
Leek Road,
Stoke on Trent

> Peter and Jenny Lister
> work so hard, and their
> welcome is always
> genuine and
> wholehearted.

Ian Gregory

The Manager,
The Little Chef,
Norton,
Evesham.

> They did not complain
> when I changed my mind
> after ordering ... always
> politeness and patience.

Mrs. J. H. Cook

Lockers Greengrocery and
Nursery,
Council Car Park,
Cheadle,
Cheshire

> Kind and willing to take
> trouble over every need

Miss Annie Weston

The Post Office,
Cheadle,
Staffordshire

> Very patient and
> prepared to take a lot of
> trouble with each
> customer.

Mrs. Evelyn Bree

Waitrose Ltd.,
1-6 Sir George Mall,
Kidderminster.

> Everybody is so helpful
> and the service is so good
> that it is a pleasure to go
> into the shop.

Miss K. M. Pitt

G.L.Foster,
Fosters General Drapers,
81 Market Street,
Ashby de la Zouch,
Leicestershire

> With the help of kindly
> ladies Mr. and Mrs.
> Foster run this Olde
> Worlde family shop ... so
> helpful and obliging.

Mr. and Mrs. K.W.L.
Pepper

S. J. Buckley Esq.,
Bratts Butchers,
Sandy Lane,
Brown Edge,
Stoke on Trent

> Always respectful,
> friendly and obliging.

O.A.Kelsall

Machins Jeans Shops,
30-36 Peveril Street,
Nottingham.

> A shop in a million for
> consistent excellent
> service, friendliness and
> always the utmost care
> and consideration.

Mrs. Patricia
Wardman

Staffordshire Building Society,
High Street,
Albrighton,
Wolverhampton.

Cheerful manner to all

J. Evans

The Piano Workshop,
Yoxall Lane,
Newborough,
Burton on Trent,
Staffs.

Careful and detailed attention. They go out of their way to give excellent service.

Polite Society Inspector

Exhibits and Flowertime,
9 George Street,
Newcastle, Staffs.

The owners of this shop are untiringly helpful and generous. Nothing is ever too much trouble for them.

Anne Burdon

Rackhams Store,
Parade,
Leamington Spa,
Warwickshire.

Acted speedily and politely over a problem. In every department helpful kindly and polite staff.

Mrs. R. McGuire

Doctors' Surgery,
136 Brunswick Street,
Leamington Spa,
Warwickshire.

Excellent, friendly and cooperative service to the general public.

Polite Society Inspector

John Ingall Esq.,
19 Station Road,
Long Eaton,
Nottingham.

I put a notice outside my shop saying that we took trouble to say please and thank you. The response was terrific and made my business really great. Customers could see from outside that they would be spoken to correctly. It just shows what can be done by being polite.

John Ingal – whose move inspired the courtesy enterprise scheme

Building Society Shop,
Advanced Business Centre,
City House,
Maid Marian Way,
Nottingham.

I have always received prompt and courteous attention.

Mrs. Mary Stone

154

Doctors' Surgery,
23 Bridge Street,
Burton on Trent,
Staffordshire.

Among the friendliest
and most polite group of
receptionists I have ever
met. Telephone manners
are excellent. Waiting in
the surgery is a pleasure.

Mrs. C. M. Mills

Birds Cakes,
St. James Street,
Derby.

I am an ex-serviceman
and now a supplementary
pensioner, and I was
brought up to be
courteous. I regularly
shop here and it is always
service with a smile: they
are most helpful.

Mr. A. Foster

Park View Surgery,
26-28 Leicester Road,
Loughborough,
Leicestershire.

Enquiries reveal this to be
a popular and well
appreciated practice,
carrying out a valuable
service to the community
with skill and devotion.
Receptionists excellent.

Polite Society Inspector

N. Clarke Esq.,
Post Office,
Hyson Green Post Office,
52-54 Gregory Boulevard,
Nottingham.

Beautiful people who
treat everyone with
kindness, courtesy and
consideration

Miss Dolores Behrman

Stakis Grand Hotel,
66 Trinity Street,
Hanley,
Stoke on Trent.

In spite of busyness,
thoughtful and most civil
attention

Polite Society Inspector

Pennington Lee Ltd,
8 Balaclava Road,
Derby.

No quibbles: no extra
charge for work done ...
courteous treatment.

Miss I Butler

R and E Steele
Tobacconist and confectioner
Lad Lane
Newcastle under Lyme

Old-fashioned standards
of splendid courtesty.

R. Gabriel Gregory

Basford Post Office,
Etruria Road,
Basford,
Newcastle under Lyme.

> Personal service and
> cheerful acceptance of
> the thousands of Polite
> Society mail items each
> year. Deep gratitude.
>
> *Ian Gregory*

Weston Park,
Stately Home,
Weston Lizzard,
Staffs.

> Unusual and superb
> level of welcome and kind
> greeting from all staff.
>
> *Miss K. Waite*

Corporation Bus drivers,
Nottingham.

> Wonderful, kind,
> considerate people.
>
> *Dolores M. Behrman*

Aroma Centre,
Watergate Arcade,
Whitchurch,
Shropshire.
> *Trisha Gregory*

NatWest Bank,
Leek Road,
Endon,
Staffs.

> Recommended by.
>
> *Audrey Kelsall*

Edward Ward,
Postman,
Barston,
Solihull,
West Midlands.

> Known as Eddie, he has
> been the jpostman for
> this area for at least 20
> years. He is always
> cheerful, chatty, smart,
> reliable and thoughtful.
> Always checks house
> during vacations and
> closes gates securely.
> Makes time to stroke and
> chat to my dog although
> she can be ferocious and
> at first used to lie in wait
> for his hand as it came
> through our floor-level
> letter box. (He never
> mentioned what it did to
> his back!) For at least 12
> months he has had to
> clamber across planks,
> through mud and loose
> bricks, but he has never
> complained, while we
> have neen extending our
> house . . .
>
> *Mrs. Helen A.*
> *Williams*

156

Boulton Street Garage
Northwood
Stoke on Trent

> Derek Nealings and
> Bryan Aldridge merit a
> mention in the Good
> Manners Guide

> *Audrey   Kelsall*

David I Frudd Contractors Ltd
69/73 Liddington Street
Basford
Nottingham

> Exceptionally good
> mannered, kind and
> wonderfully helpful

> *Dolores   Behrman*

Borough Arms Hotel
Kings Street
Newcastle
Staffs

> Thoughtful and well
> managed hotel,
> restaurant and bar
> provision.

> *Polite Society Inspector*

George and Dragon
High Street
Newcastle
Staffs

> Cheerful banter and well-
> judged real life humour
> make this a deservedly
> popular pub.

> *Polite Society Inspector*

Diana Lucy Fashions,
Cavendish Arcade,
Buxton,
Derbyshire.

> . . . particularly helpful to
> large women, often
> treated with contempt in
> other clothes shops . . .
> cup of tea if you look tired
> . . .

> *Mrs N. Scott*

The Opera House,
Buxton,
Derbyshire.

> Under administrator Mr
> Christopher Grady the
> staff are unfailingly
> helpful. All queries are
> answered in full and with
> interest . . . the utmost
> polite attention.

> *Mrs N. Scott*

Patons (Shifnal) Ltd,
Motor sales and service,
Cheapside,
Shifnal,
Shropshire.

> Staff are always so polite
> and welcoming that it is a
> great pleasure to be a
> customer. Although I live
> in Hertfordshire I have
> my car serviced at
> Shifnal. Proprietor and
> staff obviously put the
> customer first.

> *Dr. Dorothy M.*
> *Derbyshire*

The Icing on the Cake,
Cake decorating supplies
Trinity Street,Worcester;
Regent Arcade,
Cheltenham;
The Royal Priors,
Leamington Spa.

> Knowledgeable, helpful,
> courteous and above all
> they smile when they
> serve a customer.
>
> *Liz Brooks*

Fred Boyn,
Head porter,
Robinson College,
Cambridge.

> Really helpful and
> friendly even to lowly
> students like me.
>
> *Nicola   Macdonald,*
> *Matlock*

Poppins Restaurant,
29/31 Georege street,
Oxford.

> Highly commended.
>
> *Patricia M. Wharton*

Mansfield Inns Ltd have engaged in a thorough training scheme for some 2,000 members of staff at 100 of their public houses. Personnel Manager Richard Marrion invited the Polite Society to assess the affect of the training programme, and our inspectors have no hesitation in commending the sample seven public houses which they visited:

Rampant Horse, Hall Road, Orchard Park Estate, Hull

Duke of Cumberland, Market Green, Cottingham, North Humberside

Elephant and Castle, Holderness Road, Hull

Sir John Cockle, Sutton Road, Mansfield, Notts

Reindeer Inn, Southwell Road West, Mansfield

Black Bull, Woodhouse Road, Mansfield

Three Lions, Netherfield Lane, Meden Vale, Mansfield

Polite Society

Courteous Communities

1987

Shrewsbury
Newton Stewart

1988

Norwich

Nominations welcomed for future Awards

EAST

Prontaprint,
High Street,
Lincoln.

Each member of staff I
have dealt with has
been unfailingly
courteous even when
under pressure.

C.S.Polak

R.E.Thorns and Co.,
Hardware,
22 Exchange Street,
Norwich.

Only too pleased to
recommend them

Mrs.B.Yarrow

Max Snedden,
Garage Manager,
Serviceman,
BR Car Park,
Peterborough.

Impressive courtesy.

*Peterborough Evening
Telegraph staff*

C.C.Clements Ironmongers,
Fairland Street,
Wymondham,
Norfolk.

Over many many years
a consistent friendly
service to all

E.Mead

Librarian,
The Library,
Bury St. Edmunds,
Sergeants Walk,
Bury St. Edmunds.

Staff are patient and
pleasant and willing to
take endless trouble to
help and listen instead
of giving the impression
that we (the public) are
interrupting a very busy
person with more
important things to do

Mrs.R.Bates

J.J. Falkus,
Station Road Stores,
28 Station Road,
North Walsham,
Norfolk.

Friendliness, kindness
and cheerfulness –
trouble.

R. and D.M.Pizzey

Tricia and Colin Stephenson,
Natural Food Store,
4 Exchange Street,
Norwich.

We had several letters
about this shop. One
from Mrs.M.Thorne
said:

Small in size but huge in
help. The nicest kind of
shop to go into; they
always cheer me up.

J.J. Yates Esq.,
The Black Horse,
Swaffham Bulbeck,
Cambs.

Mr. and Mrs. Yates'
pleasant and caring
attitude towards all
callers is outstanding.

B.Geoghegan

M.J.C.Prentice Esq.,
Scotts Butchers,
High Street,
Castle Camps,
Cambridgeshire.

Always a welcoming
smile and greeting.
Unfailing good advice.

Mrs.Aideen Tudenham

Beehive Butchery,
51 Cannerby Lane,
Sprowston,
Norwich.

Five young men, always
smiling, humorous and
polite to all age groups.

Mrs.S.Welch

Station Road Stores,
North Walsham,
Norfolk.

Friendliness, kindness
and cheerfulness –
nothing too much
trouble.

Mr.and Mrs.Pizzey

Michael Hope Esq.,
Wig and Mitre Public House,
29 Steep Hill,
Lincoln.

Licensee and staff make
every effort to make one
feel welcome and at
home. Cheerful and
friendly.

Polite Society Inspector

Doctors' Surgery,
Templegarth,
Tinkle Street,
Grimoldby,
Lincs.

Dr. Mansfield is a most
unusual GP, ably
supported by wife and
receptionists to give a
unique caring service

J. Lees

Texas Homecare,
London Road,
Ipswich.

Compared with all the
other DIY Stores I have
recently visited this was
the most courteous and
helpful.

N.Bannatyne

YCENI (Mind) Workshop,
Nelson Drill Hall,
Artillery Square,
Great Yarmouth,
Norfolk.

... an atmosphere of harmony and tranquility combined with a genuine businesslike purpose, hard to find nowadays...

Dr R.F. Armstrong

Post Office and Stores,
High Street,
Monks Eleigh,
Ipswich.

Mr Arthur Sadler and his staff extend friendliness, cheerfulness and helpfulness to everyone, even children with only 10p to spend.

G.T.Warrington

Goddards,
Ladies and Gent's Outfitters,
Norfolk Street,
King's Lynn,
Norfolk.

... kind, helpful staff who always make a person feel special. Husbands are offered coffee while their wives try on clothes.

Barbara Penney

Aerolite Garage,
Norwich Road,
Watton,
Norfolk.

I am a pensioner and the kindness I receive from Mr.Parrot and his staff is unbelievable in these times – a rare breed.

Mrs.Joan Allen Burns

Holden Motors,
Off Westwick Street and
Whiffler Road,
Norwich.

Helpful, kind and courteous in looking after me, a disabled motorist, over the years.

Miss Vera E.Page

Norwich Co-op,
Magdalen Street,
Norwich.

I nominate manager Roger Drake

S.Cubitt

Sound Approach,
161 Unthank Road,
Norwich.

I nominate Martin Drake and Ian Waterson. Very good polite businessmen

F.Booth

Allen and Page Ltd.,
Quayside Mills Tack Shop,
Norwich.
>Worthy of nomination

>*Mary Ducker*
>(who also nominated the Pet
>and Garden Centre, 83,
>Dereham Road, Norwich)

Casa Fina,
Gifts and quality household
goods,
37 St Giles Street,
Norwich.

>... a genuine smiling
>welcome and interest in
>our needs.

>*F.J. Byrom*

Hungate Book Shop,
11, Princes Street,
Norwich.

>... Nothing is too much
>trouble. A genuine
>interest in your needs.

>*H.G. Smith*

Albert Sawers,
Butcher,
Market Place,
Swaffham,
Norfolk.

>... always has time to
>listen, advise and chat.

>*Barbara Penney*

Clogs and Clothes,
Plowright Place,
Swaffham,
Norfolk.

>... have time to talk and
>will always encourage
>people.

>*Barbara Penney*

Just Hair,
Station Street,
Swaffham.

>... always very polite and
>do a lot of work for
>others less fortunate
>than themselves

>*Barbara Penney*

A. J. Podolski, (Jewellers)
1 St Andrews Hill,
Norwich.

>One felt as though they
>were really glad you had
>gone in.

>*A. Brierley*

Station Road Stores,
North Walsham,
Norfolk.

>Friendliness, kindness
>and cheerfulness –
>nothing too much
>trouble.

>*Mr.and Mrs.Pizzey*

165

City of Norwich
Inquiries, housing and other
public offices,
City Hall,
Norwich.

A polite society
inspector studied the
general state of
relationships between
staff and members of
the public, and found
them to be of a very
high standard-reflecting
the training that staff
undertake in basic
communications,
getting on with deaf and
blind people, potential
problems and handling
aggression and
violence.

166

THE NORTH

Ocrixous Chemist,
(Mr.Livesey),
Dalton Square,
Lancaster.

So pleasant, cheerful
and helpful – very
unusual in any shop
these days

Mrs.Lynne Cox

Mr. and Mrs. Brown,
York House Nursery School,
York Avenue,
Crosby,
Liverpool.

I nominate 'Auntie
Shirley' for her care and
humour with toddlers

Mrs.E.E.Turner

Peter Hughes Chemist,
Longfield Centre,
Prestwich,
Manchester.

So helpful. They always
have a smile. It's a
pleasure to go in

Mrs.K.Wakefield

W.H.Smith,
The Precinct,
Birkenhead,
Merseyside.

Even in the pre-
Christmas rush they
helped me find the
books I wanted. Always
friendly

Mrs.Diana Gray

R.J.Brooks/C.H.Low,
Chartered Accountants,
Oriel House,
Oriel Road,
Bootle,
Merseyside.

Patient, pleasant and
genuinely helpful to
everybody, and
trustworthy

Mrs.B.Gorsky

Charles Stuart Menswear,
62 School Road,
Sale,
Cheshire.

Proprietor Mr.Aubrey
Hurst gives a first class
service and is a valued
member of the
community

Irving Hersh

170

Keith Donnelly,
Unit 3,
Longlands Works,
Bowness on Windermere,
Cumbria.

Motor Vehicle Repair business … I am very proud of Keith. He is honest, considerate and helpful to all his customers

Mrs.Heather Donnelly

R.W.Pollock and Co.Ltd.,
254 Barkerend Road,
Bradford 3.

Electrical sales and services. Nothing too much trouble, even when old or out of date items are taken in for repair.

John A.Stead

The Ridings Restaraunt,
508 Halifax Road,
Bradford 6.

When we have visited here staff are always polite and courteous. Absolutely outstanding in every way.

John A.Stead

Havenhand Bakery,
St. James Square,
Boroughbride,
York.

A grand bunch. Always friendly and helpful.

Mavis Hartley

Horton Motor Spares,
806 Little Horton Lane,
Bradford.

They always try and usually succeed in supplying spares for older cars

John A.Stead

Pelican Cafe,
Main Street,
Settle,
Yorks.

After a number of visits I have always found the waitresses very helpful and efficient

John A.Stead

Crockett's Dry Cleaning Service,
Bond Street,
Leeds.

A pleasure to visit this shop. Staff are so relaxed and friendly.

Mrs.Kay Fussey

Flower Box,
808 Little Horton Lane,
Bradford.

> Mr. Denis Howarth
> always has a friendly
> word for his customers.
>
> *John A. Stead*

Leeds and Holbeck Building
Society,
Oakwood Branch,
Leeds 8.

> Always polite courteous
> and cheerful
>
> *R.B.Horn*

Mrs. Barbara Salkins,
Off Licence,
71 Andrews Close,
Formby,
Merseyside.

> A very busy shop, but
> always courteous and
> look on each customer
> as an individual, and
> ready to chat despite
> pressure
>
> *Rev. Frank Cowan*

Wreyfield Shop (Fruiterer),
50 Huntriss Row,
Scarborough.

> Assistants always
> pleasant and courteous
>
> *Anne Foster*

Laxey Westminster Garage,
New Road,
Laxey,
Isle of Man.

> Service with a smile
>
> *A.Grubb*

Paul Darby Esq.,
Truffles and Quartermasters,
Cavern Walks,
Mathew Street,
Liverpool.

> Beautifully presented
> and kindly served
>
> *Polite Society Inspector*

Doctor's Surgery,
863 Ashton New Road,
Clayton,
Manchester 11

> Gentle, kind and treats
> us all as individuals
>
> *Mrs.L.Barrow*

Arighi Bianchi and Co.Ltd.,
Household Furnishers,
Commercial Road,
Macclesfield,
Cheshire.

> Not once have we been
> dealt with other than
> charmingly, and made
> to feel as if we were the
> only customers. They
> are marvellous.
>
> *Mrs.J.Burdekin*

J.E.Graham Esq.,
Formby News,
124 Church Road,
Freshfield,
Formby.

Jim supplies daily
newspapers to a house
of retirement of 29
missionary priests. He
never misses, no matter
what the wether. If there
is a delay he makes an
extra journey to deliver
to the doorstep himself
when his delivery boys
have gone to school

Rev. Frank Cowan

Mr. and Mrs. G. Potter,
Old Hall Hotel,
The Square,
Buxton,
Derbyshire.

Mrs. Potter has
improved this run down
hotel and has an
excellent staff whose
kindness and courtesy
never fail

Mrs. Nora Scott

The Traddock,
Austwick,
via Lancaster

Charming welcome.
Relaxed atmosphere.
Absolutely no
complaint.

Ian Clifton

Royal Hotel,
Ferensway,
Hull.

Splendid relaxed and
caring atmosphere

Jackie Whittaker

National and Provincial
Building Society,
21 Grove Street,
Wilmslow
Cheshire.

Charming. As soon as
you step inside there is a
cheery welcome and the
service is excellent

Mrs. Jean Duffy

P.Coopland Esq.,
Coopland and Son
(Scarborough) Ltd.,
51a Middle Street South,
Driffield,
Humberside.

A very busy shop with
efficient staff who are
always helpful, patient
and cheerful.

J.T.Duck. Life Member,
Polite Society.

173

Joplins Restaurant,
45 High Street,
Great Ayton,
North Yorkshire.

Good manners and
friendliness. Our
favourite outing

Joan Laider and four
friends

Ribble Motor Services Ltd.,
Frenchwood Avenue,
Preston.

Pleasant helpful attitude
of the drivers of mini
buses in particular
towards the elderly on
Fleetwood local services

Mrs.J.Allen

Doctors' Surgery,
58 Castle Road,
Scarborough.

Generally known to be a
caring, kind and
considerate practice

Polite Society Inspector

Strikes Gardening Centre,
Cockerton,
Darlington.

I changed my purchases
twice because of colour
match and both times I
was greeted by smiles
and good manners

Mrs. P. Rees

Royal Hotel,
Ferensway,
Hull.

Splendid relaxed and
caring atmosphere

Jackie   Whittaker

National and Provincial
Building Society,
21 Grove Street,
Wilmslow
Cheshire.

Charming. As soon as
you step inside there is a
cheery welcome and the
service is excellent

Mrs. Jean Duffy

P.Coopland Esq.,
Coopland and Son
(Scarborough) Ltd.,
51a Middle Street South,
Driffield,
Humberside.

A very busy shop with
efficient staff who are
always helpful, patient
and cheerful.

J.T.Duck. Life Member,
Polite Society.

George H. Carnall Sports Centre,
Kingsway Park,
Urmston,
Manchester.

> Every staff member has a warm caring friendly attitude, and the centre is immaculately hygienic

> *Martin-Ian Hilton*

Cafe and Takeaway,
Mauldeth Road,
Withington.

> Staff always smiling, whether you have a meal or tea and toast

> *A.Squire*

Lawshall's Market,
Mauldeth Road,
Withington,
Manchester.

> Whether buying a large joint or as I do one slice of cooked meat, service is excellent and with a pleasant manner

> *A.Squire*

Post Office,
North Reddish,
Stockport.

> Most patient, courteous: friendly remarks to all

> *A.E.Newing*

Temple Photographic Studios,
420 Prescot Road,
Liverpool 13.

> Cheryl and Norman Williams never cease to amaze me with their patience and kindness to the very young and to pensioners

> *E.Bayly*

Blackley's Chemist,
110 Mauldeth Road,
Withington,
Manchester.

> Always willing to help old people fill in forms, and still courteous if goods are not bought after examination

> *A.Squire*

Headway Hotel,
East Promenade,
Morecambe.

> Elegant comfort and courtesy from management and staff

> *Mrs.E.Tweedale*

Strand Cards and Gifts,
Eastgate Row,
Chester.

> Such courteous treatment when I was looking for a special birthday card

> *Mrs.E.D.Siddora*

Clare Clothes,
Fell View,
Eskdale
Cumbria.

Superb service, and treats
each customer as a VIP

Mrs. L. MacDonald

Kwikfit Tyres,
Waterloo Street,
Bolton,
Lancs.

Always put the customer
first and always polite

A.Binns

Top Man Fashion Store,
Basement,
19 Market Street,
Manchester.

Never have I come across
such helpfulness when
shopping. Very pleasantly
surprised by courtesy and
service

A.C.Jones

Dental Surgery,
8, Ripon Road,
Harrogate,
North Yorks.

... always show caring
good manners and
thorough treatment . . .
atmospherc always light,
happy and efficient.

Ms S.J. Stopford-Taylor

Freeman Hardy Willis,
Beaulah Street,
Harrogate.

Always ready to go to
great pains to please
customers.

Ms S.J. Stopford-Taylor.

The Surgery
110, Kings Road,
Harrogate,
North Yorkshire.

Cheerful, willing and
helpful both in person
and on the telephone.
Patience and tolerance
with a smile.

Ms S.J.Stopford-Taylor

Crossroads Garage,
Flimby,
Maryport,
Cumbria.

After buying a car I have
been back five or six
times with little problems
and after giving me a cup
of coffee they have always
fixed them. They must be
the best car people in
Britain.

Mrs Lorraine Stamper

Mr E. Lewthwaite,
Greengrocers,
The Promenade,
Arnside,
Carnforth,
Cumbria.

very worthy of inclusion

Mrs E. Bamforth

Doctors and Receptionists
The Surgery,
Hurworth,
Darlington.

... so kind and thoughtful
in every situation. I am a
retired nursing sister who
had previously been a
dispenser so I know what
I am talking about!

Gertrude Painting

J.J. Gillam and Son,
Grocers and Provision
Merchants,
51, Market Street,
Ulverston,
Cumbria.

... cannot be bettered for
genuine, sincere, good
humoured and unfailing
courtesy and
helpfulness. The same
pleasant attitude to all,
regardless of how much
they spend.

Mrs Margaret Roberts

Cole Brothers,
Bakers Pool,
Sheffield.

Old established store ...
staff always polite and
will spend time ensuring
customers find what
they are looking for.

Mrs M. Clulow

Messrs Woolworth
Stores,
Fawcett Street,
Sunderland.

Determined not only to
be polite but friendly to
our customers - and to
ourselves! After all, it can
be infectious, even to a
grumpy customer

Bob Tomkys, Manager,
and confirmed by Jan
Jacques in the
Sunderland Echo

Charles Hobson,
Gents' Outfitters,
Market Place,
Easingwold,
N. Yorks.

Unusually high regard
for the customer and his
needs.

Polite Society Inspector

SCOTLAND

Balerno Garage,
Dean Park Brae,
Balerno,
Midlothian

> ... always a friendly smile or wave, a word of welcome and excellent service.
>
> *Miss E.G.F. Nicol*

Spar Supermarket,
Blairgowrie,
Perthshire.

> Courtesy from the young lad (16) right up to the manager. I find it difficult to get to the shops, but no order is too small to deliver, in the shortest space of time.
>
> *Valerie McAllan*

John Hendry Esq.,
Hendry's Giftware,
3, Bonnygate,
Cupar,
Fife.

> Friendly and helpful staff
>
> *Polite Society life member*

The Post Office,
Shandon Place,
Edinburgh.

> Mr Fred Glidden and his staff are always most helpful and patient
>
> *Mrs M. Wilson*

J. Smith Esq.,
Watchmaker and
Jeweller,
30, Crossgate,
Cupar,
Fife.

> Mr Smith always takes a friendly and genuine interest in his customers and their needs.
>
> *Polite Society member*

J.L. Richardson,
Chemist,
6A Montague Terrace,
Edinburgh 5.

> From the pharmacist to the youngest assistant they are always friendly and helpful, having a few words of chat if the shop is not too busy. Last year when my husband was terminally ill and I could not leave the house to collect a prescription someone delivered it to me.
>
> *Mrs Janet Craig*

Bejam Shop,
Byres Road,
Glasgow, G12.

> Assistants notably friendly and knowledgeable.
>
> A triumph of personnel policy and training.
>
> *K Kerner*

180

Pieter Van Dijk Esq.,
Peebles Hydro.

Staff trained by Polite
Society. Meticulous
attention to all needs and
creative enthusiasm to
ensure guests are
content.

Mrs J. Paterson

Europcar,
26, Glasgow Road,
Perth.

... the courteous
treatment I received here
improved my sense of
confidence in driving on
strange roads in an
unknown area.

An impressed customer

Pizza Gallery,
Scott Street,
Perth.

A very busy eating place
but staff under Lisa
Monro are always
cheerful, very polite and
helpful.

Mrs J. Paterson

Peter McDonough,
Butcher and game dealer,
34, High Street,
Perth.

Always a welcome with a
smile, and courteous
service that makes their
haggis taste even better.

Ian Gregory

Rowanbank Guest House,
Pitcullen Crescent,
Perth.

Hospitality at its Scottish
best from John and Eileen
Cowan.

Trisha Gregory

The Coffee Club,
Bank Street,
Kilmarnock.

Lovely music.... Manners
of management and staff
impeccable

Mae Moody

WALES

Tyr Craig Castle Hotel,
Barmouth,
Gwynedd.

> Lovely Victorian Hotel,
> well run with friendly
> service.

Alan Grubb

Spar Groceries,
Llangoed,
Nr. Beaumaris,
Anglesey.

> 'It's a pleasure,' says Mr
> Dillon, 'to send my goods
> with a customer passing
> my home.'

Miss E.B. Griffiths (81)

Mr Pritchard,
Grocer,
Morley House,
Llangoed,
Beaumaris.

> I'm assured it's no
> trouble to deliver goods
> himself.

Miss E.B. Griffiths (81)

**Bradford and Bingley
Building Society,**
9, Queen Street,
Cardiff.

> Consistently cheerful . . .
> they always do a little bit
> more than they have to.

A. Gascoyne

**Richard Vaughan
Davies,**
Vaughan Davies Ltd.,
The Cross,
Mold,
Clwyd.

> Arranged with flair and
> imagination. Well
> planned roomy gents
> outfitters. Goods neat
> and clearly priced. Old
> fashioned and proud of
> it: service prompt and
> friendly. Visitors' book
> with unsolicited
> testamonials to courtesy
> and service.

Polite Society Inspector

British Home Stores,
Commercial Road,
Newport,
Gwent.

> Manager Mr Moon is
> extremely polite. His
> caring attitude towards
> customers is quite unique

Mrs Anne Hodge

David Morgan Ltd.,
Family Store,
20 Windsor Road,
Penarth,
South Glamorgan.

> One is greeted cheerfully
> and all the staff are
> helpful and interested.

Polite Society member

184

Penarth Photographic,
Glebe Street,
Penarth.

> Willing and helpful
>
> *Society member*

Mister Minit,
Shoe repairs,
Windsor Road,
Penarth.

> Most helpful and
> courteous.
>
> *Society member*

P. Church,
Greengrocers,
Glebe Street,
Penarth.

> Happy and helpful
>
> *Society member*

Allan Green
(Volkswagen),
Park Road Garage,
Penrhyndeudraeth,
Gwynedd.

> Highly satisfactory, with
> good service and courtesy
> at all times.
>
> *Mrs Iris Bladon*

Ian A. Bailey,
Home Maintenance
Service,
30, Colin Drive,
Rhyl,
Clwyd.

> Excellent craftsman. His
> helpfulness and courtesy
> deserve acknowledge-
> ment.
>
> *Mrs Iris Bladon*

Millet's Stores,
Wrexham,
Clwyd.

> Assistant who saw my
> disabled husband
> brought a chair at once
> and was so pleasant and
> friendly.
>
> *Mrs C. Jones*

185

NORTHERN IRELAND

Orbit Markman Ltd.,
77, Loopland Park,
Belfast 6,
N. Ireland.

> Excellent workmanship
> always supervised by Mr
> Kirk and his partner. Sent
> us bouquet and fruit on
> completion!

> *Patricia Calderwood*

A.P. Mathewson,
Pharmacist,
Queen Street,
Ballymoney,
N. Ireland.

> Owner and his staff are
> lovely people who make
> shopping there a
> pleasure.

> *Fiona Williamson*

The Polite Society Code of Courteous conduct

All we ask is that those who join keep this code in mind in all their dealings with other people . . .

> So far as it is within my power I will at all times be courteous to those with whom I have personal feelings. I accept that this includes
>
> * members of my family
> * those whom I consult professionally
> * those whom I serve in my profession or business, including clients, patients and customers
> * other drivers and road users
> * tradesmen and shop assistants
> * bar and restaurant staff
>
> As a member of the Polite Society I will exercise the maximum self-control in all situations likely to test my patience and temper.
>
> I will treat all those subordinate to me and dependent upon me with kindness and consideration.
>
> At the start of each day I will make a resolution to deal with every situation as I meet it with the utmost consideration for other people's feelings.
>
> I will be especially conscious of the need to be courteous to people whose style of life may differ from my own, such as those of a different generation or race.
>
> I will (if male) treat women with especial courtesy, observing habits of chivalry towards them.
>
> I will abstain from conduct or language likely to cause embarrassment or offence to those in whose company I am at any time.
>
> I will eschew publications, performances or social events which appear to dwell on unpleasant and vulgar subjects for their own sake, and which do nothing to advance our understanding of the human condition.

The Junior Code

The Society has many junior members, and the following junior code was drawn up in consultation with them:

1. We should think of others before ourselves.

2. We should never do or say anything that would hurt another person's feelings.

3. We should especially care for children who seem to have no friends.

4. We never leave litter in a public place.

5. We should never forget to say please or thank you.

6. We should remember table manners, and not chew with our mouths open.

7. We should not use bad words.

8. We should do as our parents and teachers tell us without question.

9. We should not talk when someone else is talking.

10. We should be kind to all animals.